Corvette

Corvette

A CLASSIC AMERICAN MARQUE

CHARTWELL
BOOKS, INC.

DEDICATION

TO JOANNE LAMM

A QUINTET BOOK

Published by Chartwell Books
A Division of Book Sales, Inc.
110 Enterprise Avenue
Secaucus, New Jersey 07094

ISBN 1-55521-462–2

This book was designed and produced by
Quintet Publishing Limited
6 Blundell Street
London N7 9BH

Creative Director: Peter Bridgewater
Art Director: Ian Hunt
Designer: Annie Moss
Editor: Shaun Barrington

Typeset in Great Britain by
Central Southern Typesetters, Eastbourne
Manufactured in Hong Kong by
Regent Publishing Services Limited
Printed in Hong Kong by
Leefung-Asco Printers Limited

Illustrations in this book are from GM's own archives
from the author's collection and from Karl Ludwigsen
Associates, London.

CONTENTS

INTRODUCTION

SETTING THE STAGE 6

CHAPTER ONE

FROM STYLIST'S FANCY TO DRIVER'S DREAM 8

CHAPTER TWO

INTO ITS OWN 22

CHAPTER THREE

CORVETTE SPORTS/RACERS 40

CHAPTER FOUR

THE 1963-1967 STING RAY 54

CHAPTER FIVE

THE LONG-LIVED STINGRAY 68

CHAPTER SIX

THE CURRENT GENERATION 94

APPENDIX

SPOTTER'S GUIDE 120

INDEX 126

ACKNOWLEDGEMENTS 128

INTRODUCTION

SETTING THE STAGE

MONTEREY 1987:
Harlow Curtice's own custom '56 leads a parade of venerable Corvette specials.

Every hard figure GM had in the early '50s made the Corvette look like a bad idea. That's not to say it was a bad car – far from it. But the chances of making a profit with a 2-seat, European-style sports car were slim indeed, and the General must have known it.

America's sports car market was limited to a very small, very elite group of buyers. Chevrolet sold two million units in 1950, while sports car builders as a whole managed to move perhaps 5000 vehicles across America.

But sports cars *seemed* hot. Magazines were filled with them. The suavest, smoothest servicemen had brought sleek coupes and roadsters back from the war and still turned heads with them. All the right people seemed to be interested – but interested and willing to buy are two very different things, a fact that's rarely lost on GM.

So the question is, *why?* Why in 1953 did General Motors tool up for, let alone expect to sell, 10,000 or more Corvettes in a matter of a few years?

Officially, the company had a simple explanation: They held that the reason sports cars had sold so poorly in America thus far had been because the only ones available were European cars built by Europeans for European conditions. A sports car tailored to the better roads, wider spaces, and traditions of comfort and luxury of the American market would sell to a much broader base.

In other words, General Motors was saying that the motorist who'd buy this car didn't even know he wanted it yet. How could he? It didn't *exist* yet. GM hoped to build a car and then create a market for it. Needless to say, that's not how it's usually done.

In reality, the decision to build the Corvette wasn't a simple profit/loss equation at all. GM knew full well the benefits that could come from a dignified failure. If the Corvette could do something toward changing Chevrolet's dowdy image, then it would be worth a little time and capital to let that happen. Should it run aground in the marketplace, the car could be quietly retired. And, to be honest, GM's decision to market the Corvette was also based a lot on wishful thinking. The movers and shakers of the company were serious car lovers, and they *wanted that car!* If they could bring such a beautiful machine to market, well, that in itself would be a triumph. They wanted to believe that there were car lovers just like themselves all across the country – ones who just hadn't

been tapped.

Had Chevy's sports car been allowed to die when the lack of public interest seemed to demand it around 1955, it would be remembered very differently today. It would have been a quick, classy, good-looking, and ill-fated image car: a sign of life from Detroit that was quashed before maturity.

There would have been no '55 V-8. No '57 Fuelie. No SS, Sting Ray, Grand Sport, Greenwood, or GTP. We'd have no RPO 684, no L88, no ZR1, *nothing*. Just a few years' worth of fascinating footnotes to the

ABOVE *The first 25 or so production cars came with domed wheelcovers. Unique Corvette spinners weren't ready yet.*

BELOW *Bob McLean placed the Blue Flame engine far back in the frame for a true sports car layout.*

history of America's oversized autos.

Of course that – to the great relief of the world's enthusiasts – isn't quite how it turned out. The irony of the Corvette story is that its main characters – men like Harley Earl, Ed Cole, Zora Arkus-Duntov, and the many, many others who've championed the Corvette for more than 35 years now – were 100% right. They had hoped and wished and felt in their guts that an American-style sports car would find an audience, and it did. There really *was* an untapped sports car market out there.

7

CHAPTER ONE

FROM STYLIST'S FANCY TO DRIVER'S DREAM

HARLEY EARL *would be a main mover in the Corvette story for many years; this is a '63 plate.*

Harley Earl first got himself noticed by building custom Cadillac bodies at his family's carriageworks in Los Angeles. Fetched to Detroit by General Motors head Alfred P. Sloan Jr., he was put to work designing Cadillacs for GM in 1926.

It didn't take the tall Californian long to settle in. Earl almost immediately whipped up the 1927 La Salle – a sensational new companion car for Cadillac. Riding on the enthusiastic reception of that design and many others, he became the head of GM Art & Colour, the very first of today's proliferating automotive design and styling departments. Before Art & Colour, the shape of a car was left to the vagaries of engineers and private coachbuilders. After its establishment, automotive design became a highly competitive skill and art.

Art & Colour grew to become GM Styling in 1937, with Earl firmly at the head. Before retiring on December 1, 1958, his influence would directly shape perhaps 50 million GM cars. At six foot four, Harley Earl was a big man, and he could be imposing when he had to. But that isn't what made him so successful. He had a keen eye for design, a superb sense of showmanship and, perhaps rarest of all, the knack for getting what he wanted out of the complex political power network of GM. In 1952, one of the things he wanted very badly was the Corvette.

Earl and the people under him tried out their best ideas through GM's Motorama shows. Motoramas were annual traveling circuses of dreamcars, production models, girls, and glitz that toured the country showing off the latest GM products. It was the event of the year for styling staff – and a good section of the public, too.

The 1951 Motorama sensation was the LeSabre, a lengthy 2-seat showcar that shook the auto world to its roots. Its superb proportions, non-stop gadgetry, and visionary good looks made it one of the most talked-about one-offs ever. It would take almost eight years for production models to catch up to its broad, low shape.

But successful as it was, Earl's big roadster left the sports-car set cold. Many of them said as much to his face – in a good-natured way, of course – and told him to do something a little more *realistic*. They wanted a sports car with sports-car proportions: one that could be driven on the street and also raced on a track.

Earl had long been a sports car fan. He'd been noticing the little devils more and more on the street, and he was well aware of their increasing coverage in the media. Furthermore, his son Jerry had acquired quite a taste for them while off at college, and the enthusiasm of his son and his son's friends did not go unnoticed. Finally, the man who shaped GM's cars was convinced that he needed a new direction after the LeSabre; another tack. And he thought he knew where to find it.

CODENAME OPEL

Earl had always liked the idea of jaunty, affordable vehicles, and he thought that was the direction in which GM design should head next. His decision was soon to be firmed up and modified by a small, American-designed sports car called the Alembic I.

The Alembic I – which had gone through a number of more attractive names before its informal showing for GM execs – began life as a surplus Jeep, but its personality was changed when a racy plastic body was applied by Californian Bill Tritt, a pioneer in the field of fiberglass boat hulls. Harley Earl was impressed with the car for a number of reasons.

The Alembic I was a showpiece of GRP – Glass Reinforced Plastic; what Americans commonly call fiberglass-technology. Naugatuck Chemicals was looking to interest Detroit's automakers in fiberglass bodies, and they'd taken Tritt's car on a show-and-tell trip for that purpose. (The Alembic I failed to become the direct product of any Detroit company, but Southern California car dealer Woody Woodill did put it into kit form and limited production as the Woodill Wildfire.)

GM's executives, Earl included, were impressed with the possibilities of GRP, and the Alembic I would start them on the road that led to the Corvette's fiberglass body. But more on that later.

Earl took a liking to the Alembic I also because it was such a clean, fresh shape. And he realized that the same kind of car, with the vast resources of GM behind it, would make a real nice Motorama piece.

Earl's original thinking on the '53 Motorama Corvette leaned toward a producible vehicle in the under-$2000 range – something like the Willys Jeepster. There was by this time a growing movement to put a Motorama dreamcar into production – that is, introduce something as a dreamcar and then make

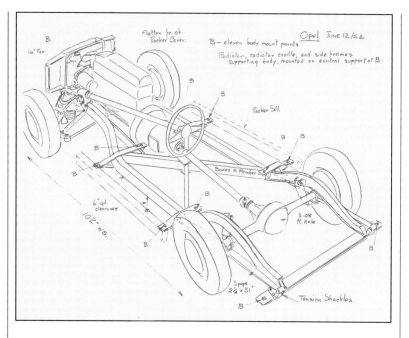

ABOVE *Maurice Olley's original sketch, from summer 1952, turned out to be remarkably close to the production frame design.*

LEFT *Not only inexpensive to tool up, engineers found GRP to be considerably lighter than steel.*

copies for the public. And the more Harley thought about the Alembic I, foreign cars like the Jaguar XK-120, and the current status of the Willys Jeepster, the more a *real* sports car was what he was after – not some big runabout knocked off an existing GM platform.

Earl assigned a young, newly-hired Cal Tech graduate named Robert McLean to lay out a small GM sports car. McLean, who had training in both

RIGHT *Every enthusiast dreams of finding a pristine '53 hidden in a barn, but with only 300 made the chances are slim.*

BELOW *Polo white, red interior, and an automatic transmission were all mandatory for 1953.*

engineering and design, was also quite a road racing enthusiast. That fact certainly wasn't lost on Earl when he handed down the assignment.

McLean's first step in the design was to break with tradition. Rather than laying down a firewall, then a cowl line, and then working outward to both ends of the car, his first move was to draw in the rear axle. He then pushed the seats as close against it as he dared, put the passengers' legs straight out in true sports car form, and went to work from there. After establishing a reasonable amount of legroom – GM designers always kept in mind the fact that their boss was six foot four – McLean dropped in a firewall, tucked in the engine as low and close to the driver as possible, and wrapped up the design with modest front and rear overhangs.

Because he attacked the design as he did, the car's engine wound up considerably lower and farther back in the frame than was normal in American cars. When questioned about the wisdom of this layout, McLean pointed out that it was exactly the way MG and Jaguar did it. That was all the convincing Earl needed.

It was simply the right way to lay out a sports car. The pushed-back engine allowed good front/rear weight distribution, a low center of gravity, and a reasonably short (102-inch) wheelbase in a low, lean, compact package. Earl gave the go-ahead to McLean's tightly knit design, knowing full well that it would never sell for less than $2000, or probably even $3000, in production form. It would need its own frame, body, driveshaft, rear suspension, and countless other parts. Each buyer would have to foot a big chunk of the tooling and development costs, and that would send the price far beyond that of anything else Chevrolet was selling at the time.

By using proprietary pieces for major components like the engine, transmission, steering, and brakes, at least the price might be kept below that of the super-exotic sports cars like Ferrari and Maserati. Almost certainly, Jaguar could be undercut as well. Yes, Earl realized, McLean's sports car would be expensive, but at least it would start out life *right*.

As head of GM Styling, Earl managed, and had absolute authority over, all the projects his staff was working on. This new sports car, undoubtedly the most exciting project at GM since the LeSabre, was one he took a special interest in.

When the shape of the body was finally laid down – with the help of McLean, designer Clare MacKichan, interior specialist Joe Schemansky, and many, many others – Earl the Showman went into action. A plaster mockup of the car was built, trimmed, and painted, and Earl arranged for Edward N. Cole – a car nut fresh over from Cadillac as Chevrolet's new chief engineer – the privilege of a sneak preview.

Cole reacted just the way Earl expected. He saw the sleek sports car and, when he finished jumping up and down and his eyes returned to their sockets, swore fealty to the cause of making Styling's car a reality. With Cole on his side, Earl knew he'd just come considerably closer to seeing the car actually in production.

Other execs would eventually be treated to surprise showings, and the "victims" invariably went

TOP Jaguar's XK-120, a fast, upmarket roadburner, turned a lot of heads. Its tucked-back engine also sold Harley Earl on the validity of McLean's design. The Maserati A6G (above) was another sports classic which must have fired Harley Earl's desire to throw a US hat into the performance ring.

BLUE FLAME *in Corvette gave 150 bhp through high compression, triple carbs, free-breathing exhausts, and long-duration cam.*

away converts – like a scene from an old Dracula movie, one more unsuspecting executive would suddenly be under the Corvette's spell.

On June 2, 1952, GM's big guns were gathered for the formal presentation of Earl's now somewhat immodest sports car. One of the men seeing it for the first time would be Thomas W. Keating, and as Chevrolet's general manager, Keating was perhaps the one man left who could still sink Earl's dreamboat. He didn't, though, and on that day Earl's little 2-seater was given the go-ahead for eventual Motorama stardom.

Suddenly, the pent-up energy of the project, code-named "Opel Sports Car," was released. Cole, ex-Rolls-Royce chassis wizard Maurice Olley, and the rest of the men who were chosen to develop the Corvette had just seven months to engineer and build a producible, running sports car for the January 17th opening of the Motorama.

It was perhaps the most ambitious project, in terms of engineering needed versus time and cash available, GM had undertaken since the war. The tight schedule would affect every aspect of the 1953–55 production Corvette, and would dictate many choices that were perhaps not in the car's immediate interest. But it did result in a car that, against all odds, was an astoundingly solid foundation on which to build the Corvette legend.

Specifications, research, prototype parts, and more began pouring out of GM at a phenomenal rate. The people assigned to building Chevy's sports car – and those doing it in their spare time or on the sly – were so enamored of the 2-seater that their work progressed at lightning speed. Within two weeks Olley had sketched what was practically the finished layout of the frame, a twin-rail unit made of box-girder sides and a central X member for strength. And he was getting the suspension and drivetrain plugged in quickly behind it.

The essentially stock Chevy front suspension sat seven inches ahead of the engine, right where Bob McLean had put it, and differed from the sedan's

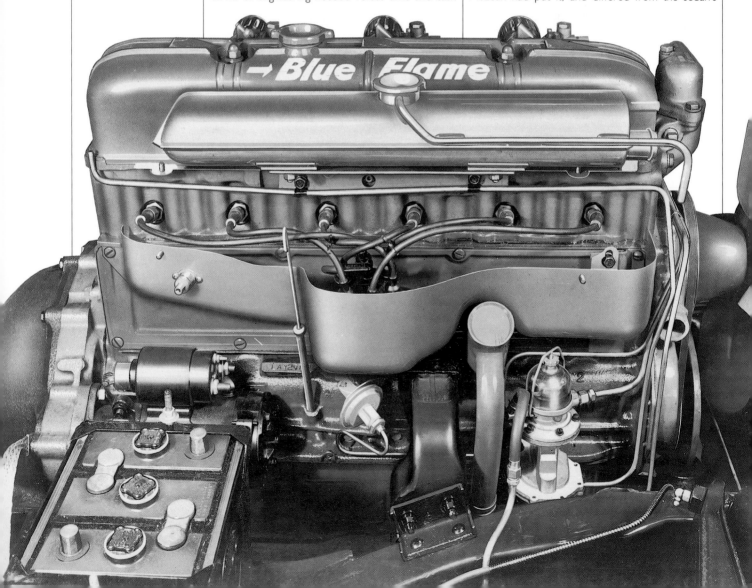

primarily in its higher placed anti-roll bar. New to Chevrolet was Hotchkiss drive instead of the traditional torque-tube, driving a live Chevy rear axle. A GM-issue Saginaw steering box was specified, its ratio quickened up from 19.4:1 to 16.0:1.

For brakes, the stock parts bin was called on again. The master cylinder was bored out to a full inch, up from the sedan's previous 7/8 inch. Line pressure was re-proportioned to take advantage of the new car's size and weight distribution. Changes to the standard 11-inch drums were put off until time would permit.

POWERPLANT

While the car's steering and stopping were being attended to elsewhere, Cole decided to tackle the engine personally. Some people feel that the '53 Corvette was doomed from the start by its use of a 6-cylinder engine, but there was quite literally nothing wrong with the Corvette's iteration of the Chev-

rolet Blue Flame powerplant. It was a well-tested engine that had received constant upgrades in both performance and reliability for almost 25 years. By 1953, it boasted four main bearings and an imminent switch to aluminum pistons. Unfortunately, the fact that Jaguar, Maserati, Aston Martin, and most other exotic sports cars did quite nicely with the same number of cylinders was lost on a lot of people.

Everyone knew, of course, that it would have been safer to launch the Corvette with a V-8 engine. And, of course, Cole would have done just that if not for one problem: Chevrolet didn't *have* a V-8 engine, and wouldn't for two more years. What they had was the Blue Flame Six.

Cole realized immediately that the stock engine's 115 bhp wouldn't be enough, but he knew that there was plenty of room for hopping it up. The first move was to bump compression up from 7.5 to 8.0:1. This meant that high-test fuel would be required, but that was literally a selling point for a performance car.

GM CALLED *the Motorama Corvette producible, and it was. Save for minor details, the production models were virtually identical.*

13

The Blue Flame's real power jump was to come from relatively straightforward but untried modifications to the cam profile, intake manifold, and exhaust system. The Blue Flame was treated to a radical (at the time) camshaft, dual valve springs with shortened, strengthened exhaust valves, and a 5000-rpm redline. Three Carter sidedraft carburetors fed the engine through a unique intake manifold. (Sidedrafts were mandatory to clear the car's low hoodline, and they looked racier than downdrafts anyway). The carbs were fitted with automatic chokes on the Motorama car, but manual chokes appeared for production.

The exhaust was worked over a number of times, finally appearing as a dual system which worked independently for the front and rear three cylinders of the engine.

Even with displacement unchanged at 235.5 cubic inches, Cole's hot rodding resulted in a serious

power increase: 150 bhp @ 4200 rpm and 223 lb/ft of torque at 2400 rpm. These figures compared well with the competition of the day: the dohc Aston and sohc Maserati engines of 1953 delivered less power than Chevy's revamped pushrod Six. Even the twin-cam Jaguar was only about 10 horses stronger. (That may explain why the Motorama car was listed at 160 bhp, rather than its true 150.) The best part was that while these European engines could be finicky, high-strung, and unreliable, the Blue Flame was about as finicky as a pig in a corn heap.

More than the engine choice, what was to truly alienate the hardcore sportscar set was the Corvette's mandatory 2-speed Powerglide automatic transmission. The Powerglide was, much like the Blue Flame itself, really all that Chevy had at the time. It was already strong enough to handle 150 horses; to modify the division's 3-speed manual transmission for the same amount of power would have been an

CLOCKWISE FROM TOP LEFT *Workers check and trim rear fender clips; others at MFGB, Ohio, pour resin on fiberglass mats to be pressed in dies. Final bodies, meanwhile, got built up and finished at Flint, Michigan.*

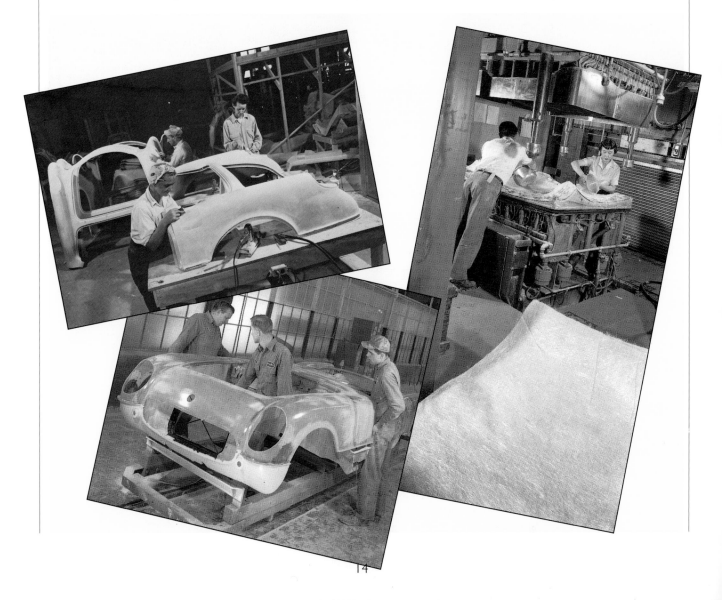

expensive proposition. The automatic also meant that a floor-mounted shifter would be simple to install, which was mandatory. A column-shift mechanism would have interfered with the rear carburetor.

Chevrolet knew that the automatic would generate flak from the sports car faithful. The sports car faithful, however, were not a big enough group to make the Corvette worth doing – remember that GM wanted to tap a much larger market.

GRP: INTO PRODUCTION

At last the car seemed ready for the Motorama. As is always the way with showcars, detail changes continued right up to the last minute, one of them being the final choice of the Corvette name, taken from a class of light French warships.

The Motorama Corvette was an unqualified, resounding success. Just as Earl had hoped and expected, the public went wild for Chevy's sleek 2-seater.

Aided by extensive media coverage, everywhere the Motorama travelled the Corvette gathered more prospective buyers. It soon appeared that Earl, Cole, Curtice, and the rest had been right: There was indeed a pent-up demand for an American-style sports car. The Corvette appealed to everyone from doctors to fishermen, although its price would plant it considerably more often in the garages of the former.

Chevy's official statements on the car alluded to its producibility, and the hints weren't lost on the public. Armed with a gigantic list of potential buyers, GM and Chevrolet decided to go ahead with Corvette production.

To avoid letting the public's fever cool any more than necessary, GM had to get the first models out with all due speed. Toward that end it was decided that the first 300 cars would be built, beginning in June of 1953, with fiberglass bodies.

Fiberglass – officially GRP – was chosen originally just to fill in while tooling was being prepared for steel-bodied Corvettes. The steel would be stamped out by Kirksite dies, dies that are cheap to produce but wear out after about 10,000 units.

But the public soon made it clear that they had no objection to fiberglass bodies – quite the opposite, in fact. Caught up in the dawn of the jet age, they were enamored of all things new and high-tech. Here was a new super material that was lightweight, rustproof,

dent resistant, easily repaired, and, best of all, completely synthetic! Rather than scaring buyers off, fiberglass appeared to be attracting them.

GM had already been looking long and hard at fiberglass bodies, and it seemed that any troubles with them could be easily overcome. Ellis J. (Jim) Premo was Chevy's top body engineer, and his experiments confirmed that GRP bodies could be put into production.

There were four methods of GRP body production for GM to choose from. The first was the simplest, and they'd already used it for styling exercises and showcars. This was the hand lay-up method, in which resin-impregnated fiberglass was simply laid into a female mold and allowed to harden.

Hand laying was the simplest and cheapest way to build GRP bodies, but it had a number of drawbacks. Most important of these was the amount of time it took to create a single panel – work had to stop while each piece sat in the mold and cured, which could take 24 hours with larger parts. Hand laying also created a panel that was smooth only on one side; the exposed inner panel remained rough and matted.

Another method was called the vacuum-bag process. Like hand laying, vacuum-bag production needed just one mold. The wet fiberglass was laid inside it and then a plastic bag was sealed around the mold's upper surface. The air was then pumped out of the bag and atmospheric pressure did the rest: the smooth bag was pushed against the fiberglass, forc-

WITH THE CORVETTE'S *arrival the old Customer Delivery Garage in Flint was suddenly a sports car factory.*

ing it into the mold and giving it a fairly nice texture on both sides. It was a simple and elegant process, but unfortunately still quite time-consuming.

The third possibility was the pressure-bag system. Pressure-bag production required a male and female mold to be made, between which resin and glass would be laid. A bag was then inflated above the male mold, forcing the two together and making a very smooth, accurate part. The disadvantage here was that the process was quite a bit more expensive than either single-mold method, while not being all that much faster.

Finally, there was matched-metal-die production. In this process again, two molds were needed, but they were quite precise and forced together like the dies for metal stampings. Matched-metal molds were the most costly and time consuming to produce, but they had the fastest cycling time and gave the most professional and consistent results. Curing time could be accelerated by circulating hot water or steam through the metal of the dies.

Robert S. Morrison, a Ford dealer-turned-fiberglass manufacturer, was eventually given the contract to go ahead with construction of a plant to produce Corvette body panels by the matched-metal process. Morrison's Molded Fiber Glass Body Company immediately began work in Ashtabula, Ohio on the $4 million contract. The details of the contract stipulated that parts for 300 bodies be delivered in 1953 and up to 10,000 each year afterwards.

Because the production time for matched-metal molds would take considerably longer than Morrison had before delivery was to begin, he sub-contracted

ABOVE *With Corvette production running in St. Louis, variations like the slick Corvair fastback could be seen at Motorama.*

RIGHT *1954/5 Corvette in Sportsman red.*

with Lunn Laminates to produce the first panels using the vacuum-bag method. As the tooling for Morrison's matched-metal parts then became available, Lunn would stop producing that piece. The larger the piece, the longer Morrison's molds took to build, and it wasn't until July of 1954 that Lunn retired from the picture completely.

General Motors' pilot assembly plant in Flint, Michigan, actually glued together, painted, and finished the pieces. Occupying a single floor of the old Customer Delivery Garage in Flint, the first Corvette production line was just long enough to build three cars a day. The Flint operation was temporary – it was supposed to run just long enough to iron out the car's bugs, which it did, before production moved in earnest to St. Louis, Missouri. The size and capacity of the Flint lineup dictated that all the cars produced there be the same color: white with red interiors.

After the first 300 Corvettes were constructed at Flint the Corvette moved to its new home. St. Louis would remain the source of all production Corvettes for nearly 40 years, until Bowling Green, Kentucky, took over production in June 1, 1981.

By 1954, full-scale production of Corvettes was a reality. Coming out of St. Louis in ever-increasing numbers, the car was offered with whitewall tires, clock, outside mirror, and automatic transmission for a retail price of over $3000. With assembly quickly coming up to speed, the great experiment began in earnest.

Chevrolet dealers had 20,000 inquiries on file, and in September of 1953 they began making small steps toward filling them. By the end of the '53 model year, only a little more than half of Corvette's 300 cars had been sold, but this had been expected: The few dealers lucky enough to get a Corvette were holding onto them as showroom traffic builders, rather than turning them loose with no replacement in sight.

With so many people apparently interested in the Corvette, Chevrolet instituted what remains a very controversial policy. They decided that the first cars were to be sold only to VIPs in the dealer's community. Politicians, high-ranking military men, actors, and other celebrities would be allowed to drive away in a Corvette immediately. Plainer folk would be denied the car until production could make some kind of inroads on the perceived

instead that leaky tops and drafty sidecurtains were by no means the sole province of the Europeans.

Chevrolet had also alienated much of the sports car set with the Corvette's automatic transmission, imitation knock-off wheelcovers, and other Detroit touches. That had seemed a reasonable price to pay to tap the much bigger market they felt Corvette had in store, but they hadn't counted on the weight that the opinion of the MG and Mercedes crowd carried. Their derision of the Corvette as a boulevard cruiser turned off many prospective buyers who, in reality, wanted just that. Magazine testers found the car's handling and performance excellent: "... on the usual two-lane, winding, road nothing *now* [a

reference to the upcoming Thunderbird] made in Michigan will touch it. The car corners with gyroscopic steadiness," said MOTOR TREND. Despite that sort of review, Corvette-bashing by fanciers of European cars took a considerable toll on the car's public image.

Meanwhile, those who *were* attached to the Corvette as an American-style sports car found its side curtains, cantankerous top, and marginal ventilation unsatisfactory. They were particularly put off by the unlockable, inner-latch-only doors. Chevrolet was caught in the middle of two camps, and the 2-seat dreamcar looked as though it could quickly turn into a nightmare. By the end of the '54 model run, 1076 cars – more than a quarter of the world's Corvettes – remained unsold. Grumblings from GM's ever-hungry accountants grew louder every hour. Worse still, Chevrolet had made no secret of their expectations for the Corvette. Falling far short of their goal was not only costly, it was embarrassing.

Production was slashed at the MFGB plant in Ashtabula, which had just gotten up to full speed. Plans for a facelifted '55 model were shelved soon

ABOVE *The 1954 Motorama starred a Corvette hardtop, Corvair fastback, and Nomad, all hiding here behind a production '54.*

ABOVE RIGHT *Corvair – unrelated to a later production Corvair – might have been produced if Corvette roadster sales had been better.*

demand. Corvette distribution was controlled with an iron hand by the Chevrolet Central Office.

But by the time that production did catch up, toward the summer of 1954, Chevrolet began to get a glimpse of their sports car dream going sour. The VIPs lucky enough to be chosen began foreshadowing the feelings of the public at large: many had cooled off considerably on the idea. They were turning Corvettes down. Even with Chevrolet's full-speed gear-up for production, the mystique and freshness of the Motorama dreamcar had begun to fade.

And those VIPs who had honored their original requests to buy were taking delivery in the dead of winter. They had pictured themselves cruising top-down through the days of summer, but were finding

after they appeared because GM decided to restrict its spending on the car – and, though no one would admit it, because they knew a new bodystyle would make the leftover '54s virtually unsellable. If money were to be spent at all on the Corvette, and that point was open to debate, it would go into the car's other upgrade for '55: a V-8 engine.

SALVAGING THE DREAM: V-8

Ed Cole and Maurice Olley were distressed by the Corvette's slow sales – distressed but not dormant. Although the Corvette's future was anything but assured, letting it lie idle while GM's bean counters sharpened their axes would only hasten its demise.

When he joined Chevrolet in 1952, Ed Cole inherited a partially completed V-8 project from his predecessor, E. H. Kelley. Kelley's V-8 wasn't advanced enough to suit Cole, the man responsible for the superb Cadillac ohv V-8 of 1949. Cole found Kelley's engine too heavy for its displacement, and felt it had insufficient room for future development and displacement boosts. In the summer of 1952, the Chevy chief engineer and right-hand man Harry Barr set to

work on an all-new Chevrolet V-8. Their design called for, and developed, a highly precise casting technique to allow much closer internal tolerances than the competition was using. The result was a powerplant that was small on the outside but spacious internally; one that had plenty of room to be let out.

With displacement initially pegged at 265 inches, the legendary small-block Chevrolet V-8 was born. Advanced casting wasn't its only forward-thinking feature; far from it. It also used stamped-steel rockers – an idea Pontiac had worked out – for their light weight and low cost. It mounted these rockers on individual studs, rather than on a shared shaft, for the same reasons, and made the studs press-in, rather than threaded, for ease of manufacturing. Hollow pushrods brought oil up to the rockers straight from the lifter galleries. The sum total of these and other parts was quite probably the best passenger-car powerplant in history.

Chevy's production small-block wouldn't come on line until 1955, but a prototype had already been shoehorned into at least one early Corvette – possibly the Motorama car itself. It demonstrated the impres-

THE INTRODUCTION *of colors – blue, red, and black – in '54 couldn't relieve sagging sales, but it was a start.*

19

sive capabilities of a V-8 Corvette, and the result was a standing order for Cole's new V-8 in the '55 model.

A 3-speed manual transmission was being tailored to accompany the new engine, and that, too, would drop in with a minimum of fuss. Here at last was a combination that would go a long way toward silencing the "purists" who called the Corvette less than a true sports car. (The manual gearbox came on line quite late in the 1955 production run – supposedly no more than 25 were actually built.)

But to see the V-8, Corvette would have to first survive its depressing '54 season. The wolves of GM's accounting department prowled St. Louis, but in the end they had to go home hungry.

SAVED BY THE COMPETITION

And then came The Scourge of Dearborn – The Ford Motor Company. Ford chose 1955 to introduce the Thunderbird, their own version of the American sports car. The T-Bird came in distinctly on the luxury side of the Corvette's sport/luxury combination. It promptly sold like gangbusters: 16,155 units moved off the production line in 1955 alone.

BELOW *Nomad dream car from the '54 Motorama; in comparison with the Corvette, more of an undisturbed night's sleep than a dream.*

BOTTOM A BRACE *of '54s take to the banks for a publicity still. GM had plenty to spare for such stunts.*

When the first Thunderbird mockup was shown to the public on February 20, 1954, Chevrolet had no idea Ford's 2-seater would do so well. But they did know there was no way they'd leave arch-rival Ford alone in a market, even if that market seemed like a sinking ship. The T-Bird raised the competitive ire of Chevrolet, and its success merely pushed new-found resources into Chevy's sportster.

Fortunately, when the Corvette was at its bleakest hour, Cole's V-8 was there to keep the momentum going. The switch to V-8 power was relatively simple – actually a bit lighter than the Six, Cole's engine

presented few problems in the sports car's engine bay. And its performance was startling: 0–60 now came up in 8.5–9.0 seconds, two seconds faster than before. Quarter-mile times were similarly improved. Better still, the Turbo-Fire Corvette would blow off the Thunderbird in virtually any form of competition driving.

With the redesign cancelled, the only obvious outer change to the '55 was a large golden "V" in the "Chevrolet" script on its side. This came with all cars equipped with the new Turbo-Fire V-8, as Cole's engine was called, and these accounted for 99% of the 700 Corvettes built in 1955.

But 700 units was another dismal sales showing, even more disappointing than the awful year before. Part of 1955's slow sales was due to Chevy's sell-off of unsold '54s, and part was due to the popularity of the Thunderbird. Those, of course, were not satisfactory excuses to GM's accountants. 1955 sales were so bad, in fact, that the 1956 Corvette entered its final planning stages just as it looked to many like a lost cause.

For those who couldn't see beyond the bottom line of the year-end budget, the Corvette was by this point a complete and unmitigated failure. But to those who had a more realistic picture of the industry, the Corvette *concept* had vindicated itself. It had certainly spearheaded a change in Chevrolet's image, from dowdy sedanmaker to that of the racy, advanced division responsible for the Corvette, the '55 Chevy, and the Turbo-Fire V-8.

THOUGH SLEEKER, *lighter, and better handling than Ford's steel Thunderbird (below), Corvette got trounced in showrooms.*

More than that, with a V-8 the Corvette was beginning to turn around the opinions of the sports car set. That, Chevy now realized, was critically important to word-of-mouth sales. Finally, the T-Bird's success not only proved the 2-seater concept, it effectively prevented Chevy from leaving the market without losing face.

The V-8 Corvette would run circles around the Ford, and with a little of its luxury thrown in, might topple it in the showrooms as well. The decision was made to give the Corvette the ammunition it needed to survive. Now all that remained was to put the pieces together and build the car that Earl and Cole had foreseen all along.

CHAPTER TWO

INTO
ITS
OWN

The chrome teeth of a '59.

1956 marked the first major body change since the Motorama Corvette's debut in 1953. It also marked the introduction of a much improved car.

Even though it had been quite successful in 1955, the 265-cid Turbo-Fire V-8 boasted a long list of improvements. Compression was bumped from 8.0 to 9.25:1. A new intake manifold carried a single Carter 4-barrel, giving 210 bhp @ 5200 rpm. An optional setup using two 4-barrels gave 225 bhp and 270 lb/ft of torque. Finned aluminum rocker covers now made the optional 225-horse engine look as special as it was, and ignition shielding was improved to prevent radio interference. An oil filter was added (1955's engine had overlooked that). A dual-point distributor was adopted to give stronger sparks to the uprated engine.

ZORA ARKUS-DUNTOV

Perhaps even more important to enthusiasts than the refinements to the V-8 was the widespread availability of the 3-speed manual transmission. This gearbox, now standard rather than optional, proved to be a delight despite its non-synchro first gear. A choice of rear-axle ratios – 3.70:1 standard and 4.11:1 or 3.27:1 optional on manual cars – tailored cruising and acceleration abilities to the needs of the individual driver.

Also much improved for '56 was the car's high-speed handling. A Belgian-born engineer named Zora Arkus-Duntov had come aboard to work on the 'Vette in 1953. After taking care of some of the car's more minor details, Duntov had turned his attention to that area.

Realizing that the front end was oversteering while its rear end understeered, Zora was surprised the Corvette behaved even as well as it did. He quickly shimmed up the suspension in key spots, altered the rear spring hangers, and generally got things set up correctly. Duntov, forever fiddling with the car's internals, would soon become the central figure of the Corvette program.

In the interior, too, the Corvette was thoroughly improved. Gone were the drafty side curtains. The car now sported roll-up windows with optional power lifts. Outside door locks and handles were specified to replace the previous car's interior-only handles. The folding top was improved mechanically and visually, and an optional power system raised

and lowered it automatically. For those wishing to forget the soft top altogether, Chevrolet offered an optional fiberglass hardtop. (The hardtop and roll-up windows first appeared on an otherwise stock Corvette in the 1954 Motorama.) Further interior improvements were a dealer-installed seatbelt package and a factory fresh-air heater.

Outside, the 1956 Corvette received a thorough workover. Its headlights muscled ahead into the airflow and the tail lights became faired in, giving an aggressive, crouching stance to the rear end. Two powerful-looking bulges flowed down the hood mimicking the Mercedes 300SL, which was sometimes also credited as the inspiration for the forward-swept headlights.

Also new for 1956 were the scalloped coves behind the Corvette's front wheels. These depressions would become a Corvette hallmark for the next seven years. Their true roots are murky, however, and somewhat in dispute.

Officially, Chevrolet took this cue from the 1955 LaSalle II and Biscayne dreamcars, both of which featured scooped-out sides of one form or another. In truth, the scoop-sided look must have come from myriad sources: Frank Kurtis' 500M and some Italian designs were already exploring it in the early '50s.

The '56 Corvette, however, was the first – perhaps the only – car to really get the shape *right*. While the concave scoops looked tacked on on most of the cars that got them, the Corvette's were so well done they could be highlighted with a chrome strip and contrasting colors.

What Chevrolet now had was simply one of the best sports cars in the world. It had a gorgeous new body, much-improved handling, considerable creature comforts, and one of the most potent yet tractable powertrains available at any cost. All that remained was to get the word out to the masses, and in this endeavor Chevrolet had enthusiastic help.

FIRST OUTING AT DAYTONA

Zora Arkus-Duntov, the emigre engineer, loved to race. And he was quickly becoming the driving force, so to speak, behind the Corvette program. Duntov was well acquainted with the European racing scene – he'd won two class victories at Le Mans in Porsches

ABOVE LEFT *Often called the Father of the Corvette, Zora Arkus-Duntov could more accurately be called a protective guardian.*

TOP *Great-looking 1956 redesign and V-8 power got buyers back in line.*

ABOVE *John Fitch (pictured), Zora Arkus-Duntov, and Betty Skelton were Chevy's designated speed pilots at Daytona Beach, 1956.*

RIGHT *Duntor's belief that there was a direct correlation between success on the track and success in the showroom did not waver. Here, he is behind the wheel of the SS, one of the next generation of Corvette racers (see p 41).*

Duntov acquired a '54 Corvette that had been used by Engineering to develop the '55 V-8. He added a racing-style windscreen, fitted a faired-in headrest, and began experimenting with top-speed runs around GM's Arizona Proving Grounds. Duntov quickly deduced the car's minimum aerodynamic drag, and figured he'd need another 30 horses from the V-8 to get into record-breaking territory.

Drawing on years of experience with pushrod valvetrains, Zora drew up plans for a medium-lift, long-duration camshaft. When it was ground and sent to Arizona, the results were gratifying. Duntov got his power dialed in, and he soon saw 160+ mph on the Arizona blacktop. Dynoed out to about 240 bhp, the so-called Duntov cam was technically a 1956 option – but the average buyer would be hard pressed to find, let alone purchase, a '56 so equipped.

Armed with the special cam, experimental high-compression heads, and about 255 bhp, Duntov's Corvette eventually took Daytona's quarter-mile acceleration honors and public recognition as the fastest car flat-out on the beach. (There was, in fact, one car – a Formula One Ferrari – that posted a speed one mile per hour faster than Duntov's.) The less modified Corvette of John Fitch took top-speed production car honors, and a similar '56 driven by Betty Skelton came home right behind him.

– and realized the publicity that similar competition would bring the Corvette. If he could graphically demonstrate the new Corvette's performance to the sports car crowd while Chevy's advertising men took care of the boulevard set, the Corvette might just become a showroom success.

Cole had earlier wanted to get the performance image of Chevy's '56 V-8 engine in the public eye. Duntov obliged him by taking a disguised '56 Chevrolet sedan to victory at Pike's Peak. Riding on the success of that venture, Duntov suggested taking the new Corvette after a top-speed record at Daytona Beach. Cole agreed, and plans were set in motion for the world's first serious Corvette competition effort.

GOOD COPY AT SEBRING

Not surprisingly, the revised Corvette quickly became accepted on America's road-racing courses. GM even launched its own semi-official Corvette racing program, a hasty assault on Sebring in 1956. That outing garnered plenty of experience and develop-

THE SNUG AND SECURE *hardtop was a welcome 1956 option. External door locks and handles came on all cars. (The '56 was never actually offered to the public in this extraordinary color.)*

ment but little in the way of all-out victories. The best finisher was 15th overall, but first in the GT (production-based) category.

From a publicity standpoint, the fact that the car didn't oust the exotic Maseratis and Jaguars at Sebring was less important than its presence there at all. One thing the Sebring campaign did generate was endless grist for the mill of Campbell-Ewald, Chevy's long-time advertising agency. They pounced on the Corvette's Sebring appearances and made sure that buyers around the country knew that not only had they been there, they'd won their class.

The results of all this activity – Cole's hot engine, the comprehensive comfort and convenience up-grades, Duntov's speed records, the racing successes, and the aggressive new body – were impressive. By the end of 1956, Chevrolet had sold 3467 sports cars, which, while not enough to make it profitable, was a distinct improvement over the past three years.

The '56 cost about the same as the '54, but the buyer got a considerably better machine for his money. The Corvette was now faster, more com-

CRAWFORD/GOLDMAN
Corvette raced valiantly and became the darling of Sebring, 1956, finishing first in class and 15th overall.

fortable, better looking, and almost certainly better value than just about any other sports car on the road. And, for the first time in its history, it had both feet firmly on the ground. Talk of summarily axing the Corvette became scarce.

"283/283" – THE YEAR OF THE FUELIE

Nobody ever accused Ed Cole of resting on his laurels, and 1957 would be another landmark year for Chevrolet. Cole had been promoted to Chevrolet general manager in 1956, and the chief engineer's title passed on to Harry Barr. Cole still took a special interest in the division's performance products, however, particularly the Corvette.

1957 would be remembered as the year of the Fuelie – the fuel-injected V-8 that made one horse-power per cubic inch. In truth it produced more than that: as much as 291 bhp came out of the newly punched-out 283 cid engine. "283/283" was such a good advertising tool, though, that the extra horses were just frosting to those in the know.

ABOVE *1956 brought faired-in tail lights, but the rounded trunk, a cue left from 1953's proposed external spare tire, remained.*

BELOW *Side script on the fastest 1957s spoke volumes: Fuel Injection.*

FI was (and is) a controlled, guided system that appeals to engineers because it promises more complete combustion. The more gasoline of a given charge that's actually atomized and burned, the more power and fewer emissions that gasoline is bound to produce.

For Cole and Chevy's advertising men, however, the appeal went beyond that: Mercedes-Benz powered its much-vaunted 300SLs with fuel injection, and the public saw FI as the last word in high-tech. Cole knew that Chevrolet would be entering '57 with modified versions of the same vehicles it had made in '56, while many of his competitors were bringing out all-new cars. He wanted a technological home run that would steal away some of their thunder. FI hit the ball out of the park.

By 1955, Zora Arkus-Duntov had joined up with John Dolza, the head of GM's FI program, to bring a fuel-injected Chevy to market. Dolza's tests had shown that a constant-flow system would be much more cost effective than a pulsed-flow one, and his development had progressed nicely in that direction. The real hangup at the time Duntov came aboard was how to tell the injectors how much fuel they needed to flow at any given moment. Dolza's proposed method measured engine speed and air density, compared the two, and then told the injection system how much fuel to deliver. Duntov suggested

The fuel-injection system was by no means the only upgrade from the already excellent '56 Corvette – also coming on line, for example, were three different Positraction rear axles – but it was definitely the most daring and interesting. The theoretical benefits of fuel injection were tempting: In a fuel-injection (FI) system, vaporized gasoline is not left on its own to negotiate the vagaries of lengthy intake manifolds, carburetor adjustments, and multiple sources of vacuum. Instead, vaporized fuel is squirted directly into the intake tract just upstream of its intended cylinder and immediately drawn in.

merely measuring the total intake flow and arranging for the FI to deliver a given amount of fuel as a factor. This is how the Rochester-built FI would eventually operate.

Ed Cole was eager to see FI on the entire 1957 Chevrolet passenger car lineup, not just the Corvette. So eager, in fact, that he was willing to put up with some imperfections to see that it was ready in time. Even an imperfect system, however, seemed unlikely for '57 after Duntov was seriously injured in a Proving Ground accident. Eventually Harry Barr's pleas would bring a back-braced, skirt-wearing Duntov back into limited service on the FI program, and the deadline would be met – just barely.

The results were impressive. With the standard camshaft, FI-equipped Chevrolets turned out 250 bhp at 5000 rpm. When the Duntov cam was specified, the same engine gave the highest specific output (output versus displacement) of any mass-produced auto engine in the world: 283 (conservative) bhp at 6200 rpm. Although the FI sales weren't fantastic – just 1040 buyers shelled out $450 for the system – it was an advertising coup of unmatched value. Despite being considerably less tractable at low speed and idle than the carbureted V-8, the fuel-injected engine garnered headlines everywhere. As intended, fuel injection put Chevrolet once again into the role of America's engineering leader.

TICKING THE BOXES: BACK TO SEBRING

Perhaps less glamorous but even more important, another '57 addition was an all-synchro 4-speed manual. Chevrolet engineers took the Borg-Warner T-85 3-speed, moved the reverse gear out to the tailshaft, and dropped a fourth gear into the resulting hole. This new gear was used to fill the large gap between first and second on the previous year's 3-speed.

With the optional 4.11 rear end, an injected 4-speed '57 Corvette could turn 0–60 times of 5.7 seconds. That's faster than today's Lotus Esprit Turbo, Ferrari 328 GTS, Porsche 911 Club Sport, Ford Mustang GT, or IROC-Z Camaro.

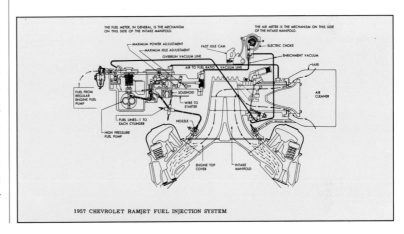

1957 CHEVROLET RAMJET FUEL INJECTION SYSTEM

ABOVE *Though simple in theory, a look inside Corvette's Ramjet FI shows injection turned out to be a tricky business.*

LEFT *Early Corvettes like the 1957 have 13 "teeth" in their grilles. The 1958-1961 models managed to get by with just nine.*

Added to the list of options for '57 was a particularly interesting item called RPO (Regular Production Option) 684. Ticking off 684 on the order sheet got you a $725 handling package including heavier springs, thicker front anti-roll bar, heavy-duty brake linings and vented drums, a Positraction (limited-slip) differential (at a mandatory $45 extra), a quick steering adapter, and firmer shock absorbers.

Finally, Corvettes came back to Sebring in 1957. This time they were better prepared. Two practice cars and three racers showed up for the event, and Dick Thompson and Gaston Andrey took one Corvette to first in GT and 12th overall. Further back in the pack was, among other things, a Corvette SR-2. The SR-2 was one of three long-nosed aerodynamic show cars built by GM for limited competition, publicity, and personal use.

Corvettes also began an 8-year series of Class B championships that year, a string which wouldn't be broken until Carroll Shelby's semi-production Cobras arrived in the early '60s. And another car made its first – and, it turned out, only – racing appearance at Sebring: the one-off Corvette SS. This purpose-built racer is discussed in more detail in the next chapter.

Corvette production reached 6339 units in '57, still short of the break-even point but climbing all the time. With the imminent departure of the 2-place Thunderbird – it was moving up in size and seating capacity – Corvette would soon have the personal luxury/sports car field as its own playground. By the end of 1957, Corvette was here to stay.

1958: CONSPICUOUS CHROMIUM CONSUMPTION

1958 found Chevy's sports car living in a slightly changed world. The original Thunderbird was gone, and the Corvette was left alone in the American 2-seater market. Fifty-eight was also the last year of Harley Earl's iron rule at GM Styling – on December 1 of that year a new man, Bill Mitchell, took over the reins as GM's chief stylist. It would take some time, of course, before Mitchell's influence would be seen on an all-new street car (due to the long lead time under which car designers must always operate).

Nineteen fifty-eight saw Detroit's chromium blitz reach an all-time high, and the Corvette was no

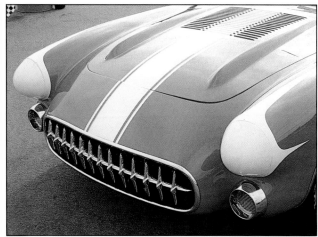

ORIGINALLY CONCEIVED
as a souped-up bomber for Harley Earl's son, Jerry, SR-2 and replicas brought Chevy tremendous publicity.

exception. Plans had originally called for an all-new Corvette in '58 rather than a redesign. Production and budget constraints killed the car before it got off the ground, though, and attention turned to the re-design proposal which Styling had been working on just in case.

The 1958 was a highly modified version of the 1956–57 shape. Quad headlights appeared, sur-rounded by chrome bezels with long spears trailing back from their centers. A fake air extractor was added to the side cove, with three chrome fingers inside for effect. Two chrome slashes crawled up the car's decklid and a washboard ridge of phony louvers appeared on the hood.

The Corvette became longer, wider, and heavier – as did nearly every American automobile in 1958. If we think today of the '58 as moving away from the sports car ideal and toward a Cadillac/Corvette hybrid, well, that's in essence just what it did. But as is so often thought, this wasn't a matter of Detroit imposing its will on the American public; quite the opposite. Americans were merely entering another phase of their romance with cars. Automakers just

IN 1958 the Corvette gained about 200 pounds, much of it in chrome. Sales took off regardless.

build what their customers want. 1958 saw new colors with the new body: charcoal, silver-blue, turquoise, and yellow. Of these it would be the turquoise, a true late-'50s color, that many people feel today best suited the late-'50s shape of the car.

There were changes inside as well. Duntov had complained long and hard about the Corvette's inte-rior, particularly the tach's placement in the center of the dash. A new layout appeared for 1958, this one putting the gauges in a cluster directly in front of the steering wheel and the tach in an individual housing on the steering column. This solution was a bit un-gainly by Duntov's reckoning, but it did the trick.

The '58 also featured a central console holding the clock, radio, and heater controls. The public had been seeing similar consoles on dreamcars for years, but this was one of their first chances to buy one.

Corvettes remained blindingly fast in '58, a fact underscored by repeat wins in the Sebring GT class and SCCA B Production racing. Chevy's most powerful FI engine was now rated at 290 bhp, the milder-cam fuelie came in at 250 bhp, and the base engine was only slightly below that with 230 bhp.

The 230-horse engine accounted for about half the cars sold that year.

Prices were up for the new quad-headlight car, but so were sales. With 9168 '58s built, the Corvette was quickly approaching the magic 10,000 mark that GM had dreamed the original Powerglide version would attain. Though falling a but short of the projected '58 sales, even the cost of the fiberglass redesign wasn't enough to keep the marque from actually turning a profit that year. That fact, if nothing else, makes the '58 Corvette a milestone.

BRAKING DOWN

By 1959, Detroit's chromium fever was beginning to abate. The Corvette's trunk trim was quietly removed, as were the fake hood louvers. Inside, the door panels were modified slightly in the form of repositioned door knobs, and the famous T-handle reverse-gear lockout made its first appearance on the 4-speed.

Perhaps the most telling change for '59 was the manner by which the rear axle was located: Radius arms trailed back from the frame and attached to the axle, counteracting its desire to chatter under hard acceleration. RPO 686 also came on line in response to racers' long-standing criticism of the Corvette braking system.

The Corvette's brakes were always a sore point at GM. While the regular finned drums on most cars were more than adequate for normal driving or even performance street driving, they tended to overheat and fade severely in competition. Racers were constantly after GM to go to heavier-duty brakes.

EARL'S LAST HURRAH, *the 4-headlight Corvette, drew customs like this XP-700 lookalike (left) in droves.*

IMPROVING *the rear-axle design and brake packages made 1959's Corvette the best driver yet.*

Likewise, the heavy-duty braking packages which GM did eventually develop for competition were wholly unsuited to street use. When they were cold their hard shoes pulled, chattered, and displayed all sorts of other rude behaviour. Street drivers who insisted on the heavy-duty brakes from Chevy's option list invariably wound up complaining that there was something horrendously wrong with them.

RPO 686 was the solution, at least for the time being. In 686, multi-layered, sintered-metallic linings acted upon unfinned drums, the insides of which had been machined and polished to an exceptionally smooth finish. The result was a braking system which behaved quite acceptably while cold, yet was still capable of hauling the heavy 'Vette down from top speed time and again.

THE END OF THE Q

For a while it seemed as though 1960 would bring a revolutionary new passenger-car line to Chevrolet, and an equally revolutionary Corvette with it. The car sailed under the Q-Body designation and centered around a transaxle being developed in the latter half of the '50s.

The transaxle – a combined transmission and axle – and the Q-Body's other high-tech features allowed GM Styling to come up with a very sleek, radically different Corvette proposal for 1960. The Q-Corvette was penned as a very compact, very light coupe. Extensive use of aluminum and high-tech hardware achieved a dry weight about 750 pounds lighter than the then-current car.

While the Q-Corvette would eventually fall victim to its own high-tech nature – it called for dry sump lubrication, an aluminum engine, inboard rear brakes, independent rear suspension, steel platform frame, and many other prohibitively costly parts – it did get the ball rolling for the Sting Ray racer and the '63 Corvette.

Bill Mitchell's influence was strong in the Q-Ship, and it would have no doubt been one of the greatest sports cars of all time. It would also, of course, have cost the GNP of a fair-sized country to design and produce. When things seemed to be turning sour for

ABOVE *Corvette was an accepted status symbol by the end of the fifties; publicity stills like this one targeted wealthy buyers.*

LEFT *Performance never slackened: racing 1957 (silver) has nothing on Le Mans-spec 1960 (white).*

the auto industry in early 1958, any thoughts of such a radical project were quickly scotched.

Regardless of the Q-Ship's demise, some of its thinking would indeed influence the '60-model Corvette. The program had gotten Zora Arkus-Duntov thinking in terms of aluminum parts for production, and aluminum heads, an aluminum radiator on some Duntov-cammed cars, and aluminum clutch housings all were planned for 1960.

The alloy heads ran into trouble early in production and were cancelled. There was nothing wrong with the parts themselves; it was the technology for manufacturing them that needed work. The alloy clutch housing and radiator were kept on line.

Corvettes broke the magic 10,000 mark for the first time in 1960, and the engine seemed, at first, to

BIG ANTI-ROLL BARS
and mild spring rates gave the '60 fantastic ride and handling. Production broke 10,000 units for the first time.

have topped 300 bhp: 315 horses were advertised for the top-line powerplant with aluminum heads. After the heads were cancelled, though, horsepower reverted to 1959 figures: 250 and 290 bhp.

Duntov then turned his attention to the car's ride, which he felt had become rather harsh in response to the needs of racing. He attacked the problem of body roll from a different direction than before, calling on large anti-roll bars front and rear rather than forever stiffening the car's springs. This solution was successful, and the smoother-riding '60 Corvette handled as well as or better than the '59.

An interesting sidelight to the 1960 Corvette story involves Chevrolet's low-key assault on Le Mans that year. Four cars made the grid, three of them prepared by Alfred Momo and some select Chevy per-

1961 *brought the Mitchell ducktail (left) to production, but the XP-700 showcar (below) was the first official GM product to wear it.*

sonnel; the other from the Camoradi team. The three Momo cars, run by Briggs Cunningham, featured ported big-valve heads, Halibrand knock-off mags, oil coolers, and myriad less sophisticated tweaks including the removal of much chrome. Piloted with great bravado by John Fitch and Bob Grossman, one of these Corvettes managed to place eighth overall, first in GT.

BILL MITCHELL

1961 brought a heavily revised Corvette to the fore, and one that for the first time reflected the design leadership of someone other than Harley Earl. Sixty-one was the first year of the Bill Mitchell Corvette, and the man's feelings on and approach to auto design were to prove quite different from those of his former boss.

William L. Mitchell had been groomed and chosen by Harley Earl for succession to the throne of GM Styling. Unlike Earl, who worked best with waves of the hand, Mitchell was a talented artist and illustrator. Also unlike Earl, he favored light, flowing shapes with lots of creases and windsplits. His boss was more a fan of the rounded, brutish look.

Mitchell came to GM initially in 1938, moving from the Barron Collier Company, a New York-based ad agency where he'd earned recognition as

an illustrator. His first assignment was the Cadillac 60 Special, and Earl liked what he saw.

The two men were of complementary minds. There were few people who could truly say they got along with Harley Earl, and even Mitchell often wondered if he was one of them. Earl was feared to some degree by everyone, Mitchell included, but there was nevertheless an understanding and friendship between the two.

Now don't misunderstand – Bill Mitchell was a superb designer. His cars were to be as excellent for their own time as Earl's had been in his. But even Mitchell wou'd readily admit that his good relationship with Earl was a major factor in his appointment to the head of GM Styling.

When Mitchell took over the reins in late 1958, however, he was far from satisfied with his situation. At least two years of Earl designs were already slated for production. Mitchell quite naturally had a great

THE SHARK, a Mitchell showcar built in 1961, was later given a mild once-over to become the Mako Shark seen here.

desire to leave his own mark on the GM line as soon as possible, and two years was too long to wait.

Dreamcars, of course, would appear much more quickly than production models. Mitchell turned in that direction. In the summer of 1958 he assembled XP-700, a highly modified Corvette. It embodied a number of ideas that both Mitchell and Earl had been working on, the most noticeable a long, oval nose flanked by four exposed headlights. Also making an appearance was the twin-bubble plastic roof that was by then rather familiar on Detroit dreamcars.

The rear end of the XP-700, however, was something that had never before been seen outside GM's walls. A long, flat deck with a high creased beltline, a gracefully backswept tail, and a windsplit running front to back gave quite a different feel to the car than the rounded, intricate front end. It was almost exactly the rear that would grace the 1961 and 1962 Corvettes.

QUIZ TIME *for the Corvette spotter: what's wrong with this '61 (below left)? Headlight bezels should be body color, not chrome. Inside (left), the dash panels are customized and the shifter knob is an aftermarket piece.*

CERV, *or Chevrolet Experimental Research Vehicle, was a racer masquerading as a research car.*

Aside from the ducktail, Mitchell put his mark on the '61 in other ways. While Harley Earl had been a big fan of flash and chrome, Mitchell decided to simplify the Corvette as much as he could. The heavy, toothy grille gave way to a simple mesh opening. The chrome headlight bezels were painted body color (though the trailing spears remained chrome). Together with its simple and elegant posterior, these touches gave the '61 a very fresh personality.

Much later, Mitchell expressed some regret about the way he'd changed the '61 model. He came to find it slightly schizophrenic, what with the modern tail on the elderly nose. His worries aside, however, the ducktailed, open-headlight Corvettes were, and are, extremely popular with the public.

Performance was improved again, the top 0–60 times now down to an almost unheard-of 5.5 seconds flat. Cast-iron versions of the cancelled aluminum

INJECTED *360-horse engine didn't hurt 1962 Corvette's chances in SCCA Production racing.*

Bore and stroke were increased ⅛ inch and ¼ inch, respectively, and the heavy-duty aluminum bearings of the hot 283s became standard across the board. Big-valve heads appeared on all but the weakest engine offered, and the dual-quad setup was sent packing.

Replacing the dual-quad option was a single Carter 4-barrel of impressive girth. While the Carter lacked the dual-quad's visual impact, it was more reliable, stronger, and much less costly.

The new engine was a screamer and, aided by stratospheric compression ratios of 10.5 and 11.25:1, made prodigious power. The Duntov/FI combination was suddenly good for 360 bhp, 210 horsepower more than the original Corvette just nine years earlier. It wasn't long before this new powerplant was applied to racing endeavors, although it would be without any official – and surprisingly little unofficial – help from Chevrolet. The Automobile Manufacturers Association (AMA) declared an end to factory-supported competition in April of 1957 and factory-supported racing had long since disappeared. Since Corvettes had already proven the masters of SCCA A and B competition, however, the 327 merely stretched their advantage.

Racing was a punishable offense in Detroit, and Corvettes would have to fend for themselves for a while. Still, Duntov and his boys found outlets for their competitive spirit in other places. For instance, many of the Corvette's "performance" parts since the AMA ban in '58 had been aimed squarely at racing cars.

Another way they stayed in the performance field without officially racing was the CERV, or Chevrolet Experimental Research Vehicle. Introduced in 1960, the CERV was a mid-engine, open wheel, single-seat racing car that Duntov built under the guise of a research tool. He did learn quite a bit from it, of course, but mostly in the area of how to build racing cars. The CERV spent its life much like Mercedes-Benz's later C111 experimentals. It was a completely raceworthy vehicle that was never allowed to compete.

The AMA racing ban which prevented CERV from officially taking on Pike's Peak, its original goal, also affected three other Corvette competition cars: the Corvette SS, Sting Ray, and Corvette Grand Sport. These three racers make up our next chapter.

heads finally delivered the promised 315 bhp for the top-line V-8. An aluminum gearcase also came on board, and the aluminum radiator was made standard on all cars, rather than appearing just on the hotter models. By this time aluminum parts had shaved off 40 of the 200 pounds Corvettes gained in 1958.

360 BHP

Chevrolet was the honored make at the Monterey Historic Races in 1987. Corvettes of all sorts came in droves. One particularly interesting car that appeared was a Scaglietti-bodied 1961. Looking much like a Ferrari coupe with Corvette teeth in the grille, the Italian-bodied Corvette was the hit of the day.

It was the result of collaboration between wealthy Texan Gary Laughlin and Carroll Shelby. The pair sent an unknown – but very small – number of '61s to Italy, where they were rebodied in lightweight aluminum. Shed of an extra 400 pounds, the Scaglietti Corvettes were admirable, if expensive, performers.

Even without Scaglietti's help, though, the Corvette was becoming one of the world's most respected cars. Nearly 11,000 were made in 1961, highlighting the acceptance not only of Corvettes in general but of Bill Mitchell's new direction. The body cleanup went even further in 1962, with Mitchell axing the bright cove accents and the contrasting-color option. The cove's three chrome spears were replaced by convincing but equally non-functional vent screens.

The really big news for the open-headlight's last hurrah was in the engine bay, however, where the 283 was pumped up to 327 cubic inches.

ABOVE *GM began a serious custody battle when the Briggs Cunningham Museum, which held the CERV, broke up. GM lost the fight.*

LEFT *The magnificent Ramjet FI smallblock; from 1957 to 1965, it was the ultimate American engine. Compared to carbs though, FI was costly, hard to tune, and lacked low-end driveability. Rochester had solved all these problems – and come up with 375 bhp – by the time production ceased in 1965.*

CHAPTER THREE

CORVETTE SPORTS RACERS

THANKS *to loving restoration by former GM engineer Lou Cutitta, SS took rightful place of honor at Monterey Historics in 1987.*

Zora Arkus-Duntov always maintained that racing held the key to success for companies like MG, Jaguar, and Alfa Romeo. Needless to say, he was eager to bring about a Corvette racing program.

EARL'S BLUFF

But when Chevy management decided to send a team of Corvettes to Sebring in 1956 – spurred on by Duntov's speed records at Daytona Beach – the engineer was horrified. He'd pushed Chevrolet to build a series of purpose-built racing cars for events like Sebring, not dolled-up production models. A former racing driver, Duntov knew that a poorly conceived effort would be worse than none at all, and given the plans laid out for Sebring that was just what Chevrolet would get. He reluctantly began work on the project, but his involvement was short-lived.

A set of experimental disc brakes had been sent down from Detroit that GM was eager to use on the racers. Duntov was well aware of their potential benefits, no doubt more so than GM's managers. But he was equally aware of the undeveloped state of disc brakes in general and those discs in particular.

After raising Cain about the proposed brakes, Duntov was pulled off the project and John Fitch took over the team – much to the relief of everyone involved. The discs did fail eventually, and extremely heavy drums wound up fitted to the 1956 race cars. They arrived at Sebring overweight.

The Corvette of Crawford and Goldman finished first in the GT class, 15th overall. Chevrolet's PR people had a field day. They touted the Corvette as a true-blue, raceworthy sports car which, at that point, was virtually true. It just hadn't been proved at Sebring – 15th overall wasn't quite what GM had intended. Hoping to improve on that in the future, Sebring became the most important event on the Corvette's calendar.

The reason Duntov held that road cars had no place taking on racers like the Jaguar D-Type or Maserati 300S was because they were doomed to failure. Even winning the production-based GT Class – which Corvettes did from the beginning – meant coming in far behind the actual race leaders. Duntov believed that well-publicized *outright* wins with a special car were much more important than low-profile class wins with a production model.

Harley Earl agreed, and he decided to force Chevrolet's hand. In May of 1956 he acquired a Jaguar D-Type and ordered it turned into a Chevrolet racing car. Earl wanted to fit the Jag with a unique body and a Corvette V-8. When Duntov heard he hit the roof.

The scheme was not only horrifying to Chevy's engineering and marketing divisions, it was downright stupid. Or was it? These days it's agreed that Earl knew what he was doing.

Duntov expressed immediate reservations at Earl's scheme, and put together a paper telling why the Jag should be discarded and an all-new car built instead. Earl had, in effect, forced GM to get rolling on the more realistic plan of building a purely Chevrolet racing car.

SS FOR SEBRING

Work began in July of 1956 on XP-46, a slippery sports/racer built on a 90-inch (later a 92-inch) wheelbase. Clare MacKichan, the man responsible for much of the '53 Motorama Corvette's detail work,

headed the styling end of the project. After initially leaning toward the title Corvette SR-X, the sports/racer became known as the Corvette SS.

Styling's design resembled the D-Type but was much more audacious. Though many of its details would get scotched by Engineering – its exposed side exhausts, barn-door-sized fairing, and so on – the car's shape and proportion remained intact from a very early stage. Plans originally called for four copies to be built, but a lack of time and manpower cut the order to one.

LEFT *Corvette road cars didn't have a prayer against cars like the race-bred Jaguar D-type, and both Duntov and Earl knew it. It had to be all or nothing: work started on the SS.*

BELOW *The 1957 AMA racing ban kept the SS from seeing more checkered flags than these. A five-car Le Mans team never came to pass.*

THE VALUE *of competition: Magazines like CORVETTE NEWS were free publicity just waiting for the SS to happen.*

brand-new Rochester fuel injection, a unique intake manifold and exhaust system, and free-flowing aluminum heads. Tuned for reliability rather than towering output, total power dialed in at 307 bhp.

While weaker than Maserati's or Ferrari's contemporary engines, that was on par with the D-Type's output and good enough for 180 mph with Le Mans gearing. That figure was important – Le Mans was to be the car's second race.

Sebring loomed closer, but the SS was still far from ready. Duntov managed to finagle enough parts from GM to assemble a test-bed prototype – the so-called Mule – to develop the car's handling while the real SS was still under construction.

While the Mule had a rough and unfinished GRP body, the SS was being tailored in handformed magnesium, a difficult and extremely flammable metal. (It was burning magnesium bodywork that caused most of the deaths in Mercedes' tragic crash at Le Mans two years earlier.) The bodywork contributed to the car's very low (1850 pounds) weight, however, and light weight was Chevrolet's weapon against the stronger Italian cars.

The most innovative, and troublesome, part of the SS was its braking system. The best drum brakes then available, Chrysler Center-Planes, were quietly purchased and modified to suit the car. Al-Fin hubs and Cerametallix linings were chosen, an advanced and normally troublefree setup.

But the method of actuation was a radical departure from the norm, and it would prove the car's biggest problem. In an effort to prevent rear-wheel lockup before full-front braking, Chevy installed an innovative dual-servo hydraulic system. The brake pedal acted directly on the front brakes only; the rears were applied by a sympathetic proportioning system. Furthermore, rear braking forces were overriden at a certain point by a deceleration-sensitive mercury switch. While the fronts were free to continue approaching lockup, in theory the rears would remain at their full effective braking rate. Given a year or two of development, the braking system might have performed as planned. Sebring, unfortunately, was just months away.

Juan Fangio was signed to drive the SS, but as the race approached and there was still no car in sight, the Argentine asked to be let out of his contract. Originally intended to co-drive was Stirling Moss, but

Zora Arkus-Duntov, meanwhile, was charged with turning Styling's creation into a racing car. Because of the short time left before Sebring, Duntov chose to develop a tubular space frame patterned after that of the Mercedes 300SL. Duntov also picked a live de Dion rear axle over an independent setup. Both choices presented fewer unknowns.

The powerplant would, of course, be the 283-inch Chevy V-8. For the SS it was fitted with then-

Moss, too, had another offer he wasn't willing to break for an invisible racing car. Eventually Carroll Shelby got the nod and, after a respectable time, he *too* backed out. While the Chevy garage remained empty, finding top-notch drivers would be difficult.

Eventually John Fitch, who was already managing the stock Corvette team at Sebring, was asked to drive the SS. A last-minute call to Rome got his old friend Piero Taruffi to fly out for the co-driver's spot, and the driver's lineup was ready at last.

IF YOU CAN'T STAND THE HEAT . . .

Unfortunately, the car was another matter entirely. When practice rolled around, Moss and Fangio both came to see what they were missing. They were turned loose for a few hot laps in the Mule, which had an unfinished body, a less powerful engine than the SS, and 150 extra pounds. In Fangio's hands, it nevertheless broke the existing Sebring lap record. Moss, too, put in some fast laps and brought the car back to Duntov with nothing but praise.

The SS, meanwhile, was in a truck heading down to Florida from Detroit, and GM employees were still putting on finishing touches en route. It arrived at last, looking lovely with silver-blue paint and brushed magnesium cove accents, Halibrand wheels, and a well finished blue interior.

It was also, alas, wholly unraceworthy. The brakes, which had worked acceptably in the Mule, were completely unpredictable in the SS. Where the Mule's fiberglass body had insulated the engine from the driver, the magnesium SS body conducted heat right into the cockpit.

Duntov made an intensive parts-swapping effort to correct these problems, but there simply wasn't time. By the race's beginning, John Fitch knew he'd be taking an unfit car into battle. One more week would have made the SS a real contender, but Sebring wasn't going to wait for Chevrolet to get its act together. He fought the car's heat and brakes for 22 laps until an overtightened suspension bushing gave way. He then (somewhat thankfully) made the decision to retire.

Ed Cole, who'd spent the day posing for publicity shots with the SS, was more than a little upset. He ordered Taruffi to take over the car, though he couldn't have done anything to the Italian had he

refused. Fortunately for Cole, after flying 12 hours just to test-drive the Mule and watch the SS putter around the track, Taruffi was game to give it a whirl.

After a single lap he'd had enough. The second SS driver returned to the pits. "Withdraw the car," he said.

After the Sebring debacle, Ed Cole was ready to give the SS whatever it needed to win races. He began making plans for a desmodromic (springless) valve system that would allow 9000 rpm and 400 horses, about as much power as the Sebring-winning Maserati had enjoyed. Duntov, meanwhile, set about the relatively simpler task of ironing out the car's brakes and bushings for Le Mans. He was also told to build three more SS racers and rebody the trusty Mule, giving Chevrolet a 5-car team. The Corvette's date in France, however, would be rudely broken.

EXQUISITE DETAIL *and perfect finish were the hallmark – and, at least at Sebring, the downfall – of the Corvette SS.*

AMA RACING BAN

In April of 1957, GM President Harlow (Red) Curtice proposed a ban of factory-supported racing to the AMA (Automobile Manufacturer's Association). Curtice feared, and reasonably so, that Detroit's current emphasis on speed and power would draw unwanted government regulation into the automobile industry. Detroit had by and large managed to avoid that in the past. Whether the AMA ban was a sound management decision or a treasonous political sellout – both opinions flourished in '57 – its effect on Detroit's performance programs was swift and cruel. For the SS it meant an order to destroy every product but the car itself. Happily, some corners held the AMA ban in such contempt that its resulting commands were consistently bent or flagrantly broken. The SS was preserved as requested, but so was the Mule. While its handsome brother threw tantrums at Sebring, the Mule had behaved so well that no one could bear to see it crushed. For two long years it sat faithfully in a GM Styling warehouse on Twelve Mile Road, patiently waiting to be called out to play.

The SS, meanwhile, made a few more non-competition appearances before being donated to the Indianapolis Motor Speedway. It would rot in the basement of the Indianapolis Speedway Museum until Lou Cutitta, a retired GM engineer, restored it to mint condition in 1987.

BENDING THE RULES:
STING RAY

The Mule, ironically, would turn out to see considerably more action than the SS. Its story picks up in 1958, when Bill Mitchell was striving to make his own

A FULL PLEXIGLASS *canopy was fitted to SS in anticipation of speed runs and new racing rules.*

mark at GM. The first all-Mitchell street cars – rather than Mitchell-modified versions of Earl designs – were going to be the 1961 models, still years away from production. Mitchell wanted to make his statement *sooner*.

A racing car, with its much shorter lead time, was the perfect answer – except for one detail. The AMA racing ban meant he couldn't simply go to GM and ask for cash to build one.

Mitchell could, perhaps with some fancy talking and a few allies, design, build, and campaign a car with his own money. But while his salary had gone up with his promotion, it was still bound by reality. To build a competitive racing car from scratch was a task that had daunted the best minds at Chevy with GM cash behind them. William L. Mitchell wasn't likely to do better on his own.

But there was a third alternative. Mitchell knew the XP-64 Mule – the 'glass-bodied Corvette SS prototype – still languished in Styling's warehouse. Already partially refurbished for the aborted Le Mans effort, it would make an excellent platform for another Chevy-based racer.

Through no doubt sticky negotiations, Mitchell acquired the Mule, on Ed Cole's authority, for $1.00. The condition of the sale was that the car be rebodied and divorced from GM completely. Officially, it was to be Mitchell's personal weekend hobby. Officially, that is.

Neither Cole nor Mitchell believed it would really wind up that way, and a studio with GM personnel and financing was quickly set up to redesign the car. It was a brave move for Mitchell, a covert operation that could easily have brought the wrath of upper management upon his head. Even ignorant of their own involvement – GM Styling's accountants were

left to hide the program costs – the top brass later demanded eloquent excuses of Mitchell's behavior.

Larry Shinoda and Peter Brock, the man who later designed the Cobra Daytona Coupe, were put to work in a secret studio before Harley Earl had even retired. Clare MacKichan, Bob McLean, and Ed Heinzman were in on the ruse as well.

The theme of Mitchell's racer came from the cancelled Q-Corvette that he and Shinoda had recently finished. While the Q-Model had been lacking a bit in the detail department, though, the new roadster was as good looking a machine as ever rolled a wheel. Powerful fender bulges punctuated the smooth hood and deck above its high, creased beltline. A faired headrest, racing windscreen, and a sleekly curved lower body finished the shape off to perfect proportions. The car received one of those rare names that really fits: Sting Ray.

Ed Heinzman developed the curved lower body on the theory that it would suck the car to the track like an inverted airfoil. Bob McLean considered that theory poppycock, and it was – the body did just the opposite, causing severe front-end lift. When the Sting Ray was being drawn up, however, the technology for testing either man's opinion was nonexistent. Heinzman's idea prevailed.

With the drawings finished, a body was laid up in heavy fiberglass during the winter of 1958–59. The Mule's engine – always slightly weaker than the SS powerplant at about 290 horses – remained essentially unchanged but for a set of SS-style aluminum heads. Because of the age of its design and the limits of Mitchell's wallet, the Sting Ray was never a world-beater on the track. Even perennial SCCA champ Dick Thompson's skillful driving couldn't overcome the awful brakes it was born with, or the skittish high-speed behavior Mitchell added in.

The Sting Ray was still burdened by fatal braking problems. Even when the dual-system actuation worked, the brakes themselves faded constantly. All three DNFs posted in 1959 were due to braking problems and, looking back, most people involved wish that they had gone to discs at the first sign of trouble. It would have been expensive, but worth it in the long run.

Regardless, the Sting Ray acquitted itself respectably in 1959, and two changes in 1960 made it truly competitive. The first was the replacement of the

heavy GRP body with a better finished version weighing 75 pounds less. Much-needed brake cooling vents were added this time.

The second was the removal of the old SS braking system in favor of a simple bias-adjustable setup. The brakes now lasted beyond the first few laps – sometimes for almost an entire race.

Duntov could probably have cured the Sting Ray's braking troubles, but Mitchell's car got little help from Engineering. Zora believed that GM products should be raced with full financing or not at all; he made Mitchell go it alone for the most part.

In 1960, the Sting Ray fought stirring battles in SCCA C-modified racing. Though first-place finishes continually eluded Thompson, he ran well in enough

EXPOSED PIPES *of the SS radiated heat into its cockpit. For the Sting Ray these were bunched together and insulated.*

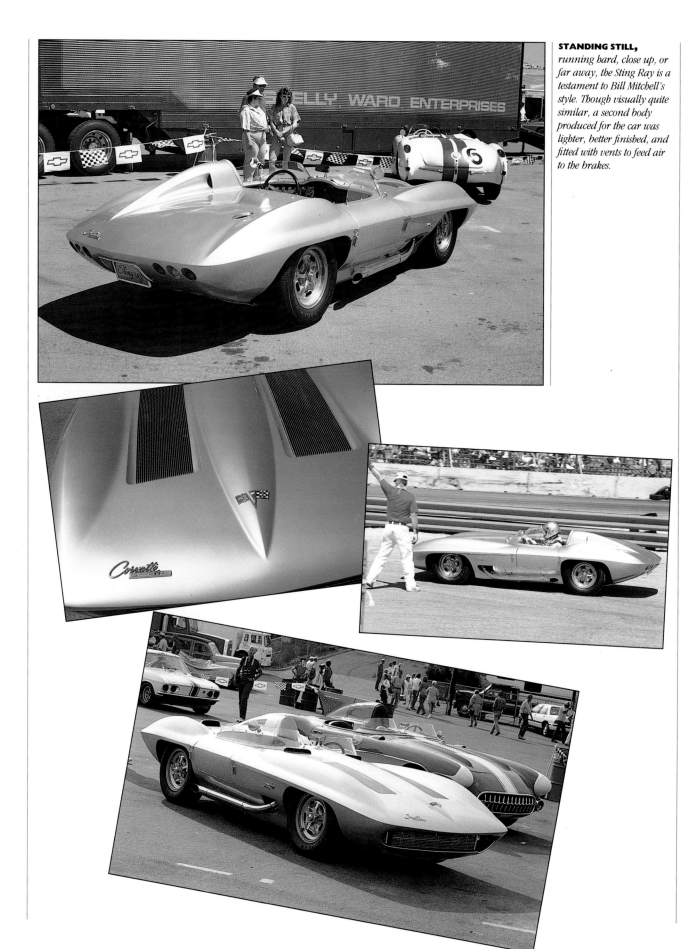

STANDING STILL,
running hard, close up, or far away, the Sting Ray is a testament to Bill Mitchell's style. Though visually quite similar, a second body produced for the car was lighter, better finished, and fitted with vents to feed air to the brakes.

LIFT AT SPEED *and weak brakes couldn't keep the SCCA C-Modified title from the World's Fastest Dentist, aka Dr. Dick Thompson.*

When the Sting Ray became too commonplace for the show circuit, Mitchell drove it as his everyday car. In time, a 427-inch engine with four Webers would be installed, as would a 377-inch small-block and Dunlop disc brakes. The car was later returned to its original specifications, and that's the way it remains today. Seen in action again at the 1987 Monterey Historic Races, it remains as beautiful and visionary as ever.

BACK TO THE TRACK WITH BUNKIE KNUDSEN: GRAND SPORT

When Ed Cole was kicked upstairs in 1960, many people felt that Chevrolet was losing its biggest go-fast proponent. But Cole's replacement, Semon E. (Bunkie) Knudsen, was just as eager to see Chevrolet products tear up the tracks as Cole had been.

Unlike Cole, however, Knudsen was prepared to butt heads with upper management to make it happen. Cole had already gone 'round the bush over Chevrolet's performance activities and been firmly instructed to back off. Knudsen, however, could claim just to be testing the limits of his new-found power.

He was certainly no stranger to doing just that. While at Pontiac, first as chief engineer and then as general manager, Knudsen and his own chief engineer John DeLorean merrily flaunted the AMA ban. Pontiac came to be associated with big-horse engines, a racy image, and back-door support of NASCAR racers.

The first thing Knudsen wanted to try in his new post, then, was getting Chevrolet back into racing. But even though Ford and Chrysler were threatening to call off their adherence to the AMA ban — which they did in May of '62 — GM was sticking to it. A frontal assault still wasn't the answer.

Zora Arkus-Duntov had cooked up a scheme, meanwhile, that his new boss just might get away with. The FIA, Europe's main sanctioning body, changed its rules considerably for '63. GT cars – cars of unlimited displacement built in numbers of 100 or more – became eligible for their World Championship. All-out sports/racing cars were limited to three liters with the idea that big-bore, production-based machines would be enticed into competition through the 100 homologation rule.

races to handily take the C-modified championship. Though C-modified was a far cry from a major world championship, it was enough for Mitchell to call himself a winner. With a title to back up its looks, his Sting Ray gamble had paid off.

The Sting Ray was welcomed back to the bosom of GM after the 1960 season. With Mitchell now holding considerable political sway it became an official Chevrolet showcar. Kenny Eschebach, an instrumental wrench during the car's racing days, added a flush tonneau cover, "Corvette" and "Fuel Injection" emblems, and a wraparound drivers' side canopy before the Sting Ray was put on display at the Chicago Auto Show in February 1961.

The Mule had made good. It now far and away outshone its refined SS sibling. By this time, it was a foregone conclusion at GM that it would be the model for the 1963 Corvette.

ABOVE *Mitchell liked taut, clean shapes without the famous Earl bulbousness. Compare this headrest to the one on the SS.*

RIGHT *Restored by Mike Begley and in its original colors, a Grand Sport returned to Nassau Beach in 1984.*

GRAND SPORTS *quite naturally figured prominently in CORVETTE NEWS' coverage of Nassau.*

Duntov's plan was simple: If Chevrolet were to construct not a purpose-built racing car but 100 production Corvettes that just happened to *run* like racing cars, where would the harm be in that? After all, it wouldn't be Chevrolet's fault if some private buyer happened to suck the doors off a Ferrari GTO with a production-model Corvette, would it?

Knudsen gave the go-ahead for 125 cars, and work began in the summer of '62. Duntov, charged

with the racer's design, skipped the high-tech monkey-motion that had caused so much grief on the Corvette SS. Instead, he chose a simple, proven layout with lots of toughness built in. Hefty steel tubes six inches in diameter were worked into a straightforward and easily produced ladder frame. Outboard disc brakes resided at all four corners, unlike the inboard/outboard drums of the SS and Sting Ray. The new transversely sprung independent rear suspension of the production Sting Ray was applied with larger rear halfshafts and a lighter leaf spring to match the car's low weight. Drilled-out trailing arms were built up from scratch, and a highly modified Corvette steering box appeared with a cast-aluminum case.

GRP would be used for the body, but very thin and light compared to the production car's. An aluminum-sheet birdcage was designed in place of the steel cage found on normal Sting Rays, and the headlights were fixed in place behind plexiglass covers rather than retractable. The Grand Sport, as it came to be known, looked much like the production Corvette but shared hardly any of its parts. The body was taller, shorter, and considerably lighter than stock, the frame and suspension were completely different, and the engine was a story unto itself.

Duntov had especially interesting plans for the GS powerplant. He took an aluminum casting of the basic 327 and added hemispherical combustion chambers, a longer stroke, strengthened rods, crank, and pistons, two plugs per cylinder, and Rochester constant-flow fuel injection. At its theoretical displacement limit of 402 cubic inches, the 16-plug engine would have produced about 600 bhp and been the strongest racing engine in the world at that time. Even at 377 inches and 550 horses, the size and power planned for '63, it had no equal.

The Grand Sport managed to avoid the scrutiny of GM's top brass until a very late date. By December of 1962, chassis #001 had already undergone testing with a 360-horse 327, and its performance was found to be promising indeed. Minor problems were ironed out, brakes refined, and everyone on Duntov's team began to taste Cobra blood on their lips. At about 2000 pounds, the Grand Sport was a half ton lighter than the normal Corvette and, significantly, 150–300 pounds less than Shelby's Ford-powered roadsters.

Once again, however, the spectre of the AMA ban rose up to quash Chevy's dreams on the eve of realization. In January of 1963, GM chairman Frederic Donner fired a memo right between the Grand Sport's (four exposed) eyes. In effect, it said that General Motors was holding firm to the ban's conditions and anyone not in agreement could find another place to work. (After being passed over for a promotion in '68, Knudsen did just that and jumped ship for Ford.)

ALL FIVE *Grand Sports still exist, and most are fitted with more powerful and modern versions of the 377-cid racing engine.*

Duntov and his crew had been able to manufacture enough pieces for just five GS Corvettes before Donner's axe fell. The potent 16-plug, hemi-chambered heads weren't among them. Those five Grand Sports were all that the world would see, giving them the dubious honor of being Chevy's highest-production "factory" road racer.

Forbidden from campaigning the cars themselves, Engineering decided to lend/lease one car each to Dick Doane and Grady Davis. These men were friends of Chevrolet who could be trusted to do their best and keep their mouths shut about it afterwards. Powered by nothing but a 360-horse 327, the Grand Sports were delivered far short of their promise and suffered accordingly.

After a year of frustrating racing in 1963, the Grand Sport Corvettes were given one chance to shine. Carroll Shelby's Cobras had creamed the stock

ABOVE *If allowed to happen, duels between Grand Sports and 427 Cobras (shown) would have been legendary.*

RIGHT AND BELOW *In vintage racing, Grand Sports can finally show their stuff without fear of starting trouble back home.*

Corvettes in SCCA racing, and the Texan spent the year rubbing it in. (Not incidentally, Shelby had originally approached Chevy for engines and had been turned down.)

By the end of the season Duntov had a bellyfull of Shelby's yakking. The two racing Grand Sports were reclaimed and a third prepared for action. Texan John Mecom was selected to head a backdoor Chevrolet effort at Nassau, the season's last race.

When the three Corvettes rolled off the boat at Nassau on December 30, they had wide Goodyears on Halibrand knock-offs, 377-inch all-aluminum engines, four twin-throat Weber carburetors, and about 485 horses of covert Chevy power. In the very first qualifier the Grand Sports blew Shelby's team into the ocean and, by the Governor's Cup finale, nothing had changed. They lapped humiliatingly faster than the Cobras, and all Shelby could do was cry foul.

Engineering's trip to the Caribbean didn't do much for Chevy, but it certainly took some of the spice out of Shelby's chili. The message was clear enough to anyone who cared to look: If GM *wanted* to go racing, the Cobras would be dead.

The coupes were in the hopeful process of being prepped for Sebring when Bunkie Knudsen was called

upstairs, chewed out up one side and down the other, and sent back to axe the GS once and for all.

Two of the five Grand Sports eventually built were converted to low-drag roadsters before they were all sold off to private owners. Roger Penske and John Mecom both bought two, and Jim Hall – the man behind the Chapparal – bought #005. The cars went through a number of owners, engines, body styles, and races in the years that followed, but never again had the factory backing that would have made them competitive. Shelby's Cobra Daytona Coupes went on to wrest the FIA Championship from Ferrari in 1965, while the lighter, better-built, and better-handling Grand Sports were left to wither as orphans.

All five still exist in good condition.

ABOVE *Ford's GT-40, here sandwiched between two Grand Sports, put the final nail in the coffin of front-engined sports/racers.*

LEFT AND BOTTOM LEFT *Robert Paterson has owned Grand Sport #003, the former Dick Doane and Nassau car, since 1973.*

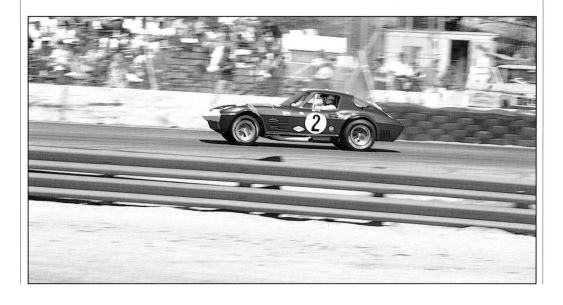

CHAPTER FOUR

THE 1963-1967 STING RAY

FAITHFUL *to Mitchell's racer, the production Sting Ray was sleek, quick and less ornamented than previous Corvettes.*

Even though the popular and advanced '57 Corvette had just begun filling showrooms, Chevrolet engineers were already working on a replacement for 1960. Two years earlier they'd put considerable effort into an all-new Corvette for 1958, but that program was cancelled as unnecessarily expensive. The Q-Corvette, their project targeted for 1960, fell to a similar fate in the winter of 1957–1958.

A SMOOTHER RIDE

It wasn't until fall of 1959 that serious work began on a second-generation Corvette that would actually see production. And noting the Corvette's steadily rising sales from 1956 to 1962, it seems that GM was correct, at least in a business sense, in carrying the first generation on as long as it did.

Regardless, by late 1959 the body of the XP-720 – the car that would become the '63 'Vette – was taking shape along roughly the same lines as the Q-Corvette before it. Mechanically it was much simpler, retaining the body-on-frame construction, GRP skins, and front-mounted engine and transmission of the previous model. All these had been in question on the Q-Car, but they were definite for the XP-720.

While the layout was similar, the '63 would be a completely different car. The only components carried over would be the engine and transmission. The frame was a ladder design with boxed side rails and five crossmembers, rather than the old car's X-braced structure. The completely restyled body sat down in, not on, the new frame. The powerplant was offset one inch from the center (crowding the passenger's side) for increased driver legroom, better one-up balance, and proper driveshaft alignment over the offset rear-axle pinion.

The axle itself was independent, unlike the old car's. To achieve the handling, ride, and stability he wanted for the next-generation Corvette, Zora Arkus-Duntov had eagerly awaited the Q-Car's independent rear suspension. When the Q evaporated, Zora wasn't willing to let the frame-mounted rear end go with it.

IRS, or independent rear suspension, offers some distinct advantages over conventional live rear axles. The most obvious boon is that road irregularities and tire attitudes affecting one rear wheel aren't transferred immediately to the other, allowing both ride and handling to be greatly improved. But equally

The fixed-roof coupe originally outsold open cars by a healthy margin. Convertibles caught up toward the end of the year.

important is the reduction in unsprung weight IRS allows.

Sprung weight is the weight of the car that's isolated from the wheel assemblies by springs, shocks, and so on. Unsprung weight, of course, is just the opposite – the weight of the tires, wheels, brakes, and associated hardware that moves up and down in direct contact with the road.

The greater the ratio of sprung to unsprung weight, the smoother a car's ride. With a live rear axle, the entire differential and axle assembly counts as unsprung weight. With IRS, the differential is mounted to the frame and its weight is sprung, rather than unsprung. IRS helped drop the Corvette's unsprung weight by 33%, and the improvement in ride quality was immediately apparent.

GM engineers under Duntov's direction designed an unusual but very effective rear suspension, using U-jointed halfshafts as the upper locating links for the rear wheels. Struts below the shafts located the hubs' bottom end, while box-shaped trailing arms controlled fore-and-aft movement. Most controversial in design was the method of springing chosen: a single transverse leaf spring assembly – used on Henry Ford's Model T – acted on both wheels.

LEFT *The creased beltline and smooth deck of 1963 Corvettes was already familiar from the 1961 and 1962 models.*

BOTTOM *The famous split window: Duntov hated it, Mitchell loved it, and GM cancelled it after one year of production.*

BLESSED WITH *all-independent suspension, a slick new shape, and raves in the press, more than 20,000 1963 Corvettes found homes.*

Cole realized that the Corvette would appeal to a broader market if it were a nominal 4-seater, rather than a 2-seater only. He ordered a 4-place proto-type made to that end.

Mitchell, Duntov, and even most of the Chevrolet sales staff were against the idea, but GM Styling and Engineering reluctantly cobbled together a stretched 2+2 version of the XP-720. It was a gawky – perhaps intentionally so – effort, and Cole eventually gave in. Extra beef had been designed into the frame just in case the stretch went through, however, and that strength remained. Some stylists also point to the '63's rather upright windshield rake as a result of the 2+2 program.

Though interior and luggage space was actually better than that of the '62 model, the new car's wheelbase shrank from 102 to 98 inches. Between the tightened dimensions and an engine set farther back in the frame, the new Corvette's weight distribution became a near-perfect 49% front/51% rear split.

Mechanically, the Corvette was shaping up to be a great car: roomy, well balanced, and smooth. And the outward look of the car was changing too.

A TRIUMPH OF STYLING

The first thing people were going to notice about the 1963 Corvette wasn't a shorter wheelbase or an independent rear end. It was the sensational body which Bill Mitchell and his boys were fitting to the new chassis. Patterned (and eventually named) after the Sting Ray racer Mitchell and Shinoda unleashed in 1959, the '63 Corvette was one of the world's all-time great auto designs. Under its new boss, GM Styling was on a roll in the early '60s: The Sting Ray, Pontiac Grand Prix, and Buick Riviera all appeared within a single year. But the Sting Ray was the best of the best – Bill Mitchell's crowning achievement.

The shape had evolved over many years. GM Styling knew that its elements would sooner or later come together in a production Corvette, but no one could have known just how successful it would be. The Q-Corvette that began it all had an unfortunate rounded roof and fussy details around its wheels and nose. The production Sting Ray would be virtually perfect.

By the time the XP-720 mockup was put on display in October of 1959, the shape was more like

Despite its age, the transverse spring turned out to be surprisingly efficient. (The current Corvette, possibly the best handling car in the world, uses it front and rear today.) The transverse spring was inexpensive, compact, and quite simply the best of the many options Chevrolet looked into.

The new ladder frame was no lighter than before, but it was stronger and less flexible. It was also shaped to allow the car's center of gravity to be lowered and overall height reduced 2.8 inches.

The frame's surprising heft was in part the result of a decision made while the new Corvette was still in its fetal stages. As Chevrolet's general manager, Ed

Mitchell's clean Sting Ray racer with the Q-Ship's roof grafted on. The car was originally seen as a coupe only, as the proposed 1958 replacement had been, but that idea was fortunately scotched by GM management.

Though the roof treatment was soon improved considerably, one feature of that first clay that did make production was a thick divider down the rear window. The divider incorporated a windsplit that ran from the windshield header to the lip of the ducktail, and Bill Mitchell absolutely loved it.

EVEN THOUGH *it was entirely new under the skin, the 1963's skin alone would have been enough for many buyers.*

Duntov and Mitchell were destined to go around and around over the so-called "split window" coupe. The engineer felt buyers had a right to see out of the back of their cars; the designer felt the bar was integral to the overall design. In an oft-repeated quote, Mitchell told Duntov "If you take that off, you might as well forget the whole thing."

In the end, both men won. The window split went into production but was summarily removed in 1964. These days split-window coupes are fairly rare – owners often took a hacksaw and removed the bar themselves.

Also contributing to the car's sleek design was its lack of exposed headlights. Hidden headlights were nothing new at the time – in fact quite the opposite: they were positively prehistoric, not having been seen since the 1942 De Soto. A number of proposals were put forward before the final rotating-nose design was settled on. Mitchell's designers tried flaps, bugeyes, and all sorts of other tricks, but the rotation idea remained far and away the best.

Making it work was another matter. Five different mechanical treatments were explored, and none was completely satisfactory. The method finally chosen used two modified electric window motors and made the car's nose a little wider than Styling had wanted. It was the best idea of the lot, but it still had problems; one of which was the manual override knobs hidden deep within the pointed nose. When the electric system failed, owners found that fiddling with the override knobs was only slightly worse than driving with no lights at all.

In December 1960, a red convertible and a silver coupe of the proposed '63 were mocked up and put out for official GM review. With a few minor exceptions, they were the shape that would see production. The coupe featured a hatchback design that allowed the entire deck to be raised for trunk access, but the hatch was later scotched for cost reasons. Both prototype cars had gas caps on their fenders – in production, the fillers were hidden under a badge on the deck.

The prototypes also had open vents in their hoods. These were Duntov's version of Mitchell's split window – a good idea that didn't work so well in practice. Engineering was eager to get radiator air exhausted through the hood, as it had been on Mitchell's racer, for aerodynamic and cooling reasons. Late prototype tests showed, however, that hot, dirty air leaving the hood grilles went straight into the cowl-mounted interior ventilation systems. If nothing else, Zora Arkus-Duntov was a man who immediately owned up to his mistakes. The vents were made non-functioning in production.

The most striking difference between Styling's late-1960 mockups and the final production versions was their decorative side vents. The prototypes had slatted scoops in the trailing edge of the door, startlingly similar to the ones used 25 years later on the Ferrari Testarossa and certain customized Porsches.

They were thankfully dropped in favor of the production car's handsome vents behind the front wheels.

PRESS SUCCESS

Once all the details of the new body were worked out, three handbuilt prototypes – a coupe and two convertibles – were made to be flogged around the GM Proving Grounds. Flog them Duntov did, and the results were impressive. The new Corvette was improved in virtually every area: handling, braking, performance, interior size, top speed, you name it.

ABOVE *More rational than Mitchell's racer, the production '63 was still quite radical to most drivers.*

BELOW *Mitchell commuted to work in the Sting Ray racer during the mid-1960s. Red paint, Webers, disc brakes, even a 427 appeared.*

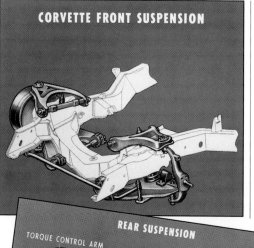

ABOVE *This was supposed to be the shape of things to come, but monorails never quite caught on like the Sting Ray.*

RIGHT *Relatively simple in design and construction, 1963's front suspension proved highly effective, regardless.*

BELOW *Transverse leaf spring and lack of upper locating links looked funny, but Duntov's IRS worked like a charm.*

BELOW RIGHT *The new ladder frame had wide-spaced side rails. Body and passengers sat in, not on, the frame.*

Through better traction, acceleration even got a boost though power and weight remained virtually unchanged. (Engine and transmission combinations were carried over with nothing more than crankcase ventilation, vacuum advance, and coolant path modifications.)

Twenty-five pre-production cars were assembled in July of 1962 on a small line in one corner of the St. Louis plant. When GM was satisfied that it could start building Sting Rays in earnest, the 25 pre-production cars were sent out for promotional duties and press intros.

REAR SUSPENSION

TORQUE CONTROL ARM

FIXED DIFFERE

AXLE DRIVE SHAFT

STRUT ROD

TRANSVERSE LEAF SPRING

1963 CORVETTE CHASSIS

It was in the summer of 1962 that writers from America's car magazines were shown the new Corvette for the first time. Chevrolet had long since learned its lesson about Corvettes and publicity, and this time the writers and photographers were circumspectly treated to an early preview. To a man, they were thrilled with the car, praising its ride, handling, and performance.

An idea of the car's abilities *as delivered*, however, would have to wait until honest production models were available. When the magazines got their hands on these for their first serious road tests, they were generous with their compliments if a bit disappointed with some minor details.

The chief culprit of these first Sting Rays was, as it always is with the first new cars off a line, quality control. Some magazines found fit and finish superb, but most got cars with bad body-panel alignment or loose interior trim. Some cars had excellent high-speed stability, while others were twitchy toward the top end. Regardless, there was a unanimous declaration that the new Corvette was a great leap forward from the old; one of the world's great performance automobiles.

THE BEST

When the 1963 Sting Rays first appeared in showrooms, buyers were faced with a number of challenges. The first was to simply get a car. Waiting lists grew to three months or more in some areas, and throughout the year buyers either paid full price or went home disappointed.

With the addition of a second shift at St. Louis and Ashtabula, cars finally became plentiful enough so that buyers could order them the way they wanted, rather than choose between what was available and a month's-long wait. They were confronted by a daunting list of options.

Offered for the first time on a Corvette were power brakes and steering, knock-off aluminum wheels (an idea suggested by Corvette racer Grady Davis), air conditioning, and a host of performance goodies including the competition-spec ZO6 package.

By year's end, production was split evenly between coupes and convertibles. More than 80% of the 21,513 1963s made were equipped with a 4-speed manual transmission, underscoring how well buyers understood the Sting Ray's sporting nature.

The most expensive option by far was ZO6, the Special Performance Equipment package intended for racing cars. Among other things, ZO6 gave you stiffer springs, bigger anti-roll bar, a 36-gallon fiberglass fuel tank (coupe only), vented heavy-duty brakes, and the strongest fuel-injected engine available. It was in this guise that the '63 went into battle.

Four ZO6 Sting Rays appeared at Riverside in October of 1962 for the Times Invitational, an accompanying race to the Times Grand Prix. They chose an odd moment to arrive on the scene, because also making its racing debut that day was a small Ford-engined roadster built by Carroll Shelby, Cobra #CSX2002.

It was obvious from that day on that the Cobra would at least temporarily end the Corvette's domination of SCCA production racing. The Cobra was built with one purpose in mind – to win races. The Corvette, meanwhile, was legitimate transportation with a roof, windows, and a reasonable amount of interior room. Since the Cobra had yet to reach three units, and would never break 1000 total, its status as a production racer was questionable. Its status as a Corvette-eater, however, was painfully obvious.

Despite losing a rear wheel and giving the ZO6 a win in its very first race, the Cobra easily walked away from the Corvettes early on. Pretty soon Shelby was bound to figure out how to tighten a knockoff nut, and then there'd be trouble. At more than a half-ton heavier than Shelby's Ford, it looked like the SCCA Corvettes were in for hard times.

CORVETTE Z06 and racing Cobra first met long before this, in October '62. Corvettes won, but the writing was on the wall.

The Cobra hurt Corvette's pride but not its sales. The two cars were made for completely different markets, and the Corvette was certainly in the more rational one. Everywhere but in the SCCA, Corvettes shone like never before. Their power had always been legendary, and that one aspect remained unchanged. Handling had been improved dramatically while the car was made more comfortable and roomier. Top speed was up a shade thanks to the low and slippery new body, and the ride was smoother on the street and flatter through the curves.

For the first time in its life, the Corvette was simply the *best*. Not just the fastest, or the most comfortable, or the flashiest, but simply the *best* sports car around. It would run with a Ferrari GT yet was as easy to live with as a Chevy sedan. It handled like an E-Type Jag but cost less than a ragtop Buick Electra.

In the next four years, it would only get better.

KEEPING UP WITH THE MUSCLE CARS

Such a good job was done on the '63 design that there were little more than minor details left to be cleaned up the following year. Many customers com-

WITH NEARLY *a half-ton weight advantage, a well driven Cobra didn't often stay behind the Z06 for long.*

plained about little things in the 1963's interior, and that was the first place Chevy looked to refine.

The 1964 cockpit environment was improved with myriad minor tweaks: the exhaust pipe mounting method was changed, for instance, to reduce vibrations sent up through the floor. Rubber bushings were put into the gearshift linkage to make the stick feel more solid. Black replaced semi-reflective silver in the gauge centers. The niggling nature of these fixes was testament to how well the car had been engineered the first time.

The Corvette was also modified in ways to make it seem more solid; more of a piece. Variable-rate springs – a technology Duntov had explored with the Corvette SS – were applied so that the ride was at once softer and more resistant to bottoming. Thicker insulation was used under the carpets to soak up some of the car's copious – and, many felt, enjoyable – mechanical noise. In the engine room, horsepower climbed to an all-time high: 375 bhp from the fuel-injected 327. But while Duntov had so far satisfied America's appetite for output with fuel injection and high-overlap cams, the times they were a-changin'. The decade of the 1960s was one of ever-bigger engines and annual jumps in horsepower.

STING RAY *brought new meaning to the term Spirit of St. Louis. Both factory morale and output soared.*

Enthusiasts' tastes shifted from refinement and light weight to brute power and blinding acceleration. The Corvette was by no means immune to this phenomenon – in fact as America's only sports car it was especially sensitive to it.

In 1965, Duntov and new Chevrolet chief engineer Jim Premo came to an agreement about upsizing the engine. Duntov had long wanted to keep the Division's W powerplant – a big, heavy V-8 introduced in 1958 – out of the Corvette engine bay. He'd by and large managed to keep the Corvette faster than America's big-engined sedans without sacrificing handling, balance, or braking to a larger powerplant.

It was obvious by '65, however, that something had to be done if the Corvette was to remain faster than big-bore monsters like the Pontiac GTO and Plymouth Super Stock. It would need more power than Chevy could reliably coax from their small-block engine. The '64–'65 Corvette's 327/375 would prove to be, in fact, the most powerful small-block GM would ever offer. Chevrolet's big-block engine for the '65 Corvette was pegged at 396 cubes. GM's internal marketing plan kept displacement under 400 inches in mid-size sedans, some of which were to share a version of the Corvette's new engine.

What appeared in the Corvette wasn't merely an updated version of the same engine Chevy'd been using since 1958. The original W powerplant had undergone a thorough reworking to become the Mark II stock-car-racing engine in 1963. Canted-valve combustion chambers gave this reworked powerplant tremendous performance and the nickname *Porcupine*, in honor of the valve stems sticking out every which way from the head.

It was from this engine that Premo whipped up the Mark IV, the powerplant introduced in the '65

Corvette. The strongest Corvette suddenly leaped 50 horses to 425 bhp, breathing through a simple Holley 4-barrel instead of costly fuel injection.

Surprisingly, the extra weight (150 pounds) up front didn't hurt handling all that much. Duntov had suspected that just such an engine swap might take place during the Sting Ray's lifespan, so he'd made allowances in the front suspension.

STYLING *of 1965 (above and 1966 (below) appeared identical save for grille, trim pieces, and the smooth 1966 B-pillar.*

The new engine required a special hood bulge to clear its aircleaner, and functioning side vents were added behind the front wheels in place of the bogus '63 and '64 vents.

Exposed side exhausts, long promised on Corvette showcars, also became available in '65. The pipes were laboriously designed by Premo to remain reasonably cool on the outside – a task that was only partially successful. Under the skin, big-block cars got stiffer springs, larger anti-roll bars, stronger axle shafts, a heavy-duty clutch, and a larger radiator.

Though the small-block Corvette was much more "tossable" and controllable through corners, the big-block was by no means difficult to drive. It went where it was told with a minimum of drama except, perhaps, dramatically fast. Still, the big-block was more taxing to live with than the 327. It ran hotter, required more muscle to steer and shift, and drank gas like it was going out of style (which, 10 years later, it was).

The big-block was really at its best only when accelerating madly in a straight line. The 327 remained the engine of choice for driving and touring – it was already very, very fast – but the Mark IV was the absolute last word if you had to win every stoplight drag you came to.

CONTROLLING THE HEAVY METAL

Besides the Mark IV engine, 1965 saw another major component change. Four-wheel disc brakes appeared as standard equipment, though you could still get drums early on as a delete-for-credit option. Production Corvettes never did offer front discs alone.

The challenges of adapting disc brakes to the relatively heavy and unquestionably fast Corvette were sizable. A number of disc suppliers had already tried and failed. Knowledge gained with the lightweight Grand Sports – they used Girling discs all around – was eventually applied to the production

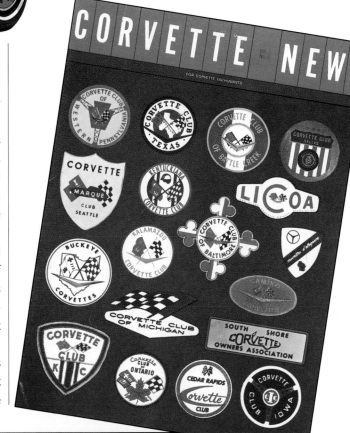

model, as was a good deal of original thinking.

The Corvette's drum brakes had become quite sophisticated by '65, but the public wanted discs. Chevrolet was considered almost backward for sticking with drums so long – even little Triumph, after all, had discs back in '55. The fact that perhaps Chevy had good reason to stick with drums was rarely considered. Despite their virtually universal use in the racing world, disc brakes were far from perfect – and the heavier the car, the worse the problems.

One of discs' biggest troubles was the extra pedal effort they required. It was obvious some form of power assist would be necessary for the Corvette's disc brakes, but GM management ruled out mandatory power brakes as too costly. Engineering was left to figure out a new way to solve the problem.

They came up with a system in which four pistons acted on pads that clamped a vented rotor (disc) at each wheel. Sixteen pistons in all gave a fair measure

A BIG YEAR *'65 was, with disc brakes, the Mark IV big block (left), and clubs filled to capacity with happy owners.*

1967 was supposed to see an all-new body, but delays meant just a minor redesign. The side vent design was unique to 1967.

By 1966, the Mark IV V-8 was in and fuel injection was out. Rochester injection had come a long way by 1965, and more than one person was sad to see it go. But the big-block was a cheaper, more reliable way to make lots more power and torque. Its size went up to 427 inches – a full seven liters – and power availability was 390 or 425 bhp. With the conservatively-rated 425-horse engine straight-line performance became stunning. Sub-13-second quarter miles could be run with trap speeds over 110 mph. Zero-to-sixty times of about five seconds were simply a matter of ordering up the 427, a close ratio 4-speed, and the 4.11 rear axle.

The 327/250 was dropped in '66 and the 327/300 became the base Corvette powerplant. The lower output 427 – if you can call 390 conservatively rated horses lower output – was offered to go with the 427/425, and this more or less filled the power niche left by the missing FI engine. Available with either a 4-speed or the (rare for '66) Powerglide automatic, the 427/390 sported an iron intake manifold and 2-bolt main bearings instead of the 427/425's 4-bolt caps.

The engine stable continued to grow in 1967, the year that the Corvette had originally been slated for reskinning. (The next chapter goes into this in greater detail.) Three 427s were offered: the 4-barrel 427/390 was the cheapest, and two 3×2s – engines with three two-barrel carburetors – took the high end at 400 and 435 bhp. Aluminum heads, as attempted on the 1960 Corvette, were offered with the L71 for $368.65, and they took 85 pounds off the front end of the car. The aluminum heads put weight and balance right between that of the 327-equipped car and the big-block, split nearly 50/50 front to rear. Unfortunately, the same manufacturing woes that plagued the heads in 1960 would make their re-appearance in 1967.

A fourth 427, the L88, was ostensibly available and ostensibly tuned for 430 bhp. At over $500 more than the 435-horse L71, the L88 got little or no interest from the average buyer. In fact, dealers were told to do whatever they could to discourage anyone asking about it.

Making the L88 even less appealing was the mandatory addition of option C48: the deletion of a heater and defroster. Just 20 L-88s were built, and as you've probably guessed Chevrolet had no desire to

of surface coverage, but Chevy's real innovation was that the pads never pulled away from the disc. When not applied, they rested ever so lightly on the rotor itself – a system now common to virtually all disc brakes in production.

This resting position allowed every bit of pedal movement to be translated directly into friction. As an added benefit, the constant contact prevented water from getting between the pad and disc and thus altering pedal response, a common ailment at the time.

The Mark IV engine and the fade-proof brakes weren't originally planned together, but their appearance at the same time was fortunate. While the drums had worked well, it's doubtful that even they were up to the task of hauling all that new-found metal down from speed. As it was, the Corvette had plenty of stop to match its increased go.

BIG BLOCK ENGINES *and disc brakes brought Corvettes back into the competitive fray after their Shelbyshock wore off.*

sell them to the public in the first place. The engine was strictly a covert racing product, its realistic output something like 570 horsepower. L88s came with 12.5:1 compression, a Holley 850-cfm 4-barrel carburetor, high-overlap camshaft, aluminum heads and intake manifold, and a strengthened bottom end. They were in no way docile enough for the street.

It was the most powerful engine Chevrolet had ever offered (nominally) to the public, and the Corvette began to march on Cobra territory despite its added weight. The final end to the Cobras would be left to the new Corvettes of 1968 and later, but 1967's L88 was an important springboard.

By 1967 the Corvette had, without any major body alterations, undergone a serious change of personality. The small-block coupe was still a nimble, rewarding driver's car, but it was by and large forgotten amidst the hoopla of the big-block's acceleration. What had started as a sophisticated sports-touring car in 1963 had become, at least in the public eye, a hairy-chested dragstrip cruiser.

That image would be reinforced through the end of the '60s and into the '70s, but Duntov's vision of a more balanced machine would be revived in years to come. For the immediate future, Corvette fans wanted neck-snapping acceleration, and that was just what they'd get. They could look forward to stronger, faster engines inside the wicked new body of the next Corvette generation.

CHAPTER FIVE

THE LONG-LIVED STINGRAY

Two years after the introduction of the '63 Sting Ray, and long before the public had tired of its unique styling, GM wanted a theme up and rolling for an entirely new Corvette for '67.

F1 WITH FENDERS

Well, not *entirely* new. Unlike the redesign in 1963, when Mitchell and Duntov had to simultaneously create and coordinate a whole new car, the '67 redesign seemed likely to affect only the Corvette's body. Much as Chevy had done to the Corvette in 1958, a new skin would give the Sting Ray the illusion of newness while relying on its time-proven platform for performance.

There *was* some talk of a mid- or rear-engined Corvette for '67, fueled particularly by the ascension of Pete Estes to the post of Chevrolet general manager in 1965. Engineers who'd been shot down previously hoped their new boss would be more receptive to this sort of pet project. But Bill Mitchell's faith was in a Sting Ray-based replacement, and that was the contingency he really planned for.

Suspecting he'd be working with the same platform as before, Mitchell's biggest problem was that his previous Corvette had been so successful. The worst thing a designer can do is propose a new model that's less attractive than the car it replaces, and it would take considerable effort to improve upon the 1963 Sting Ray.

Mitchell set down what he wanted from Larry Shinoda and his men. "Give me a Formula One car … with fenders," he told them. Shinoda, and his assistant John Schinella, drew up some baseline sketches of sleek bodies with bulging, pontoon fenders. Mitchell liked their beginnings and started hammering away at the theme.

Under Mitchell's guidance and Shinoda's pen, the fenders became fluid with the body. They still stood out as the design's main theme, however; the first thing that caught the eye.

Taken into final sketches, Shinoda's high-fendered car was an exciting shape to say the least. At the front, a low, flat hood with finned air extractors rode between two peaked fenders. The nose itself had a prominent vee like the XP-755 Shark showcar. At the rear, a high deck and a long, tapered tail created tension and a crouching stance. Best of all, it was a completely new shape.

UNLEADED FUEL ONLY

CORVETTE – *and all other makers of performance-orientated machines – were heading for a power output roller coaster over the next 20 years, with the mid-1970s as the low point, as emissions controls tightened and the oil crisis bit.*

Shinoda's drawings would become the Mako Shark II showcar. It would be as much a model for the late-'60s Corvette redesign as the original Sting Ray racer had been for the '63.

The Mako Shark II made its debut in April, 1965 at the New York Auto Show. Loaded with gadgets and legitimate looks at the future, it was an instant success with the crowds. Many in the enthusiast press, however, used it to engage in the popular new sport of Detroit bashing.

The Mako Shark II featured a removable targa roof, elaborately finned sidepipes (John Schinella put his body and soul into those), a 396 Mark IV engine, pop-up doors for the rear warning lights, and dozens of similar touches. There was no end to the details, both big and small, crammed into the Mako Shark II.

Many of them would eventually see production. The vacuum-powered panel which hid the windshield wipers was pretty whiz-bang stuff in '65, but it actually made production in '68. The Mako's clam-

LEFT Mitchell wanted "A Formula One car . . . with fenders." Shinoda and Schinella obliged him with the Mako Shark II of 1965.

shell hood saw the light of day on the 1984 Corvette. Body-colored nose and tail sections were installed on production Corvettes in 1973 and 1974, respectively, and the digital instruments which graced the Mako interior predated the production Corvette's LCD gauges by 19 years.

Two Mako Shark IIs would eventually be built, the 396-equipped, non-running New York Auto Show car, and a 427-powered driver. Distinguished primarily from the display car by its lack of elaborate sidepipes, the runner saw duty in Europe as a show-car and in America as Mitchell's personal machine.

The Mako Shark II had to be considerably tamed down before a production car could come out of it. When the time came to turn the Mako into a Corvette, Chevrolet engineers had to dictate many changes simply to make it producible. The hoodline had to be raised significantly to clear the car's mechanicals. Some form of bumper had to be applied to the nose. The Mako's quartz-iodide headlights

ABOVE *Mako Shark II took a mild reskinning to become the Manta Ray for 1969's auto-show circuit.*

RIGHT *Mako Shark I, evolved from the original Shark shown here, was shown alongside Mako Shark II during both cars' long lifespans.*

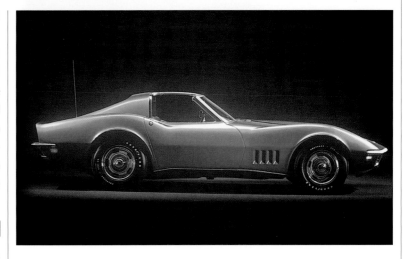

IT'S NOT hard to see the family resemblance between Mako Shark II showcar (left) and a production '68 (below).

had to be replaced with four retractable Sealed Beams.

The tail had to be most radically altered. The themes that held it together – a low roof, louvered rear window, and long, high ducktail with retractable spoiler – were unsuited to production. A talented designer named Alan Young put long hours into an all-new tail, and his skills show in the result. If anything, the rear clip of the proposed production model was cleaner and more integrated with the overall design than the Mako's original had been.

LATE RUNNER

Corvette trivia fans will have noticed by now that the new body was supposed to come out in 1967. But Corvettes didn't actually change over until 1968 – Engineering simply wouldn't let it happen. Zora Arkus-Duntov accepted the fact that styling played a big role in the Corvette's success, but he felt that the proposed '67 simply sacrificed too much function to achieve its good form.

"The car was not fit to drive on the street," he later said, citing that the front fenders were so high as to block forward vision. The deck design left the driver blind in back as well, and Duntov found the entire experience understandably disconcerting. After Duntov put his foot down, Larry Shinoda had

to do some skillful reworking of the shape before it was turned over to Hank Haga and Dave Holls' production studio. Finally, by the time everyone was pleased with the car, it was too late to be introduced as a 1967 model.

An all-new interior came along for the ride, and here again Duntov had reservations. The ancillary gauges had been moved from directly ahead of the steering wheel to a central console beneath eye level. This very clean interior theme would be in production through the 1982 model, however, and few people besides the perfectionist Duntov found fault with it.

Carried over for '68 were five engine choices: the 327/300, 327/350, and 427s with 390, 400, or 435 bhp. Actually, there were three 435-horse engines: the standard L71, the hotted-up L89, and the competition-spec L88. Also carried over was the Sting Ray's ladder frame, unchanged save for details of body and suspension mounting. A new Turbo Hydramatic transmission came on line to replace the Powerglide, and three 4-speed manuals – standard, close-ratio, and close-ratio heavy-duty – were offered as well.

Suspension changes had to be made to accommodate the new things happening on the surface. The 1968 body was about 100 pounds heavier than before, with most of the new weight right up front where the Corvette didn't need it.

Wider 7-inch wheels were fitted, and the suspension was tweaked to take advantage of their extra grip. But while the new setup improved handling, the Corvette's personality had been shifting from that of a canyon-carver to a straight-line, high-speed cruiser. Rather than appreciating the improved handling, many of the Corvette's new breed of buyers found fault with the stiffer, noisier ride that came with it.

But what really troubled the '68 was a simple lack of quality control. The big-block engine overheated magnificently, often destroying its optional aluminum heads in the process. Rain leaked into the cockpit. Doors and latches failed to work as intended. It was, for Chevrolet and Corvette, a very bleak period in what should have been a great year.

ZORA RETURNS

It didn't take Chevrolet long to realize the error of trying to integrate a machine as special as the Corvette into their mainstream engineering program. Nor did it take newly reappointed Corvette program boss Duntov – heads had rolled and a healthy Zora was called home to set things right – long to straighten the Corvette out. In the meantime, however, valuable prestige and customer loyalty had been lost.

To the public at large, fortunately, the Corvette's new body was a knockout. Despite the rough spots and poor reviews of the '68, a record-breaking 28,566 units were built. And quality woes or not, the car's performance was unquestionable – it surpassed the cornering power of the previous model and

Less debatable than the wisdom of the gauge layout was the fact that the new Corvette had much less interior space than the previous model, despite being seven inches longer overall. Mitchell's wasp-waisted design gave up the interior gains of 1963 and then some. Shoulder room was tight, and luggage space shrunk significantly.

Zora Arkus-Duntov became quite sick during the final stages of development for the '68, and he disappeared from the scene for months. During the same period, a restructuring – a shakeup, if you like – occurred within the chain of command at Chevrolet and, when Zora returned, his role in the Corvette program had been slashed. He was no longer at the head but merely a special consultant. He had no real power. The Corvette became the responsibility of the same group that engineered Chevrolet's other products, and the '68 would suffer for it. Despite its year-long final gestation, it arrived truly under-engineered.

TOP A 427 under its hood bulge, the new Corvette offered 390-, 400-, or 435-bhp engines and a wide choice of gearing.

ABOVE In part inspired by Ferrari, the flying buttress rear treatment of 1968-1977 is usually credited to Alan Young.

accelerated like gangbusters. An L88-equipped '68 with 4.11 Positraction would jump from 0–60 in less than five seconds flat, faster than anything a Corvette owner was likely to encounter.

Because of the bad reputation '68s gained early on, until quite recently they were something of a collector's bargain buy. Prices were reasonable since many buyers preferred the old-style '67 or the more refined '69. The troubles of the '68, however, were more of the annoying-but-easily-fixed variety rather than any sort of fatal flaws. A little work at home could bring them up to par with the best Corvettes of the '60s. Collectors have wised up since then, and a '68 Corvette – particularly a big-block convertible – will cost a packet now.

The '68 will have special meaning to at least one Corvette fan forever: his father's Le Mans Blue '68 convertible, with a close-ratio 4-speed and 427, was the first Corvette this author was lucky enough to drive.

When the 1969 model year rolled around, Zora Arkus-Duntov was ready. To make the car's interior more pleasant, Duntov stiffened the frame to reduce shakes and rattles. He added extra shoulder room through reshaped door panels. A smaller steering wheel gave the driver an increased sense of spaciousness and made entry and exit easier, and a new tilt option helped further still.

Overheating of the big-block engine was dramatically reduced. Zora used the plan he'd intended for

TOP *The Aero Coupe showcar presaged production features like a deep chin spoiler and body-colored nose.*

ABOVE *It takes a keen eye to spot this as a '69, not '68 model. Stingray (now one word) script on the fender is the best clue.*

KISS THE COBRA GOODBYE: *In 1969, big-block Owens-Corning Corvettes gave Chevy its first A-Production title since 1962.*

an engineer with Chevrolet's engine program, won the SCCA A-production national championship that year, returning Corvette to the head of the class it had dominated until the arrival of the Cobra in 1962. The Owens-Corning Corvette team he drove for would become one of the most successful teams in SCCA history.

1969 was an extra-long year for the Corvette. A 2-month strike led Chevrolet's new general manager, John DeLorean, to let the 1969 model run long into the intended 1970 year. A seemingly astonishing product run of over 38,500 units reflected the lengthened '69 selling season.

DeLorean realized that with Chevrolet selling every Corvette it could build, good business dictated jacking up the price. Prices for both the coupe and convertible rose about 10% for 1970 but, to be fair, it was a much-improved car. More headroom and more options were available, and tinted glass, Positraction, and the 4-speed transmission all became standard.

The exterior was treated to a modest redesign that let the neighbors know you'd bought a new Corvette and not a used one. Egg-crate side vents and grilles came aboard in 1970 and the car's appearance would remain virtually unchanged through '72.

Of particular interest to the go-fast set was the long-awaited LT-1, a solid-lifter small-block with 370 claimed horsepower. The LT-1's unique personality came through a long-overlap cam grind, and from intake and exhaust tracts lifted directly from the big-block engine.

This was, for many, the ultimate Corvette. It was delicately balanced – weight was distributed 50/50 front to rear – and devoid of the power accessories that Corvettes seemed to be sprouting more of each year. And it was *fast*. It veritably flew through the quarter-mile, clocking high 13s at well over 100 mph. The 8-inch wheels introduced in 1969 gave the LT-1 fantastic grip, and a big-block-style hood scoop gave it neighbor- as well as driver-appeal.

Under the leadership of confirmed 'Vetteophile Allan Girdler, CAR LIFE magazine had always found nice things to say about Corvettes – they gave the LT-1 a positively glowing review entitled "The Best of All Possible Corvettes." Within the first paragraph came this line: "This, chaps, is what motoring is all about." The magazine went on to talk about the LT-1

the '68 before he took ill. The holes in the forward bulkhead were plugged so that incoming air was forced through, rather than around, the radiator. That did the trick for all but the hottest days.

Big-blocks proceeded essentially unchanged for '69, but the small-blocks were stroked out to 350 cubic inches and fitted with 4-bolt main bearings. Though output remained virtually the same, torque and power figures moved down the rpm scale into more useful territory.

One addition to the engine lineup was the now-legendary ZL1, an all-aluminum version of the L88. The lightweight engine put out about the same power as the aluminum-head L88 but was 100 pounds lighter. At a mere $3000 – about 75% above and beyond the Corvette's base sticker – option ZL1 was another RPO intended strictly for the track. Officially, just two street-bound '69s were ZL1-equipped, one for Duntov and one for St. Louis plant manager George Heberling.

There's another reason that 1969 will always be remembered by Corvette lovers. Jerry Thompson, as a world-class sports car in every sense of the word – which is exactly what it was.

1970 saw the 427 stroked up to 454 cubic inches, a move to counteract ever-tightening emissions regulations. The highest output level dropped to 390 horses, although officially there was an LS-7 aluminum-block 454 good for 460 horsepower. The LS-7 was, in fact, produced in small numbers solely for the racing fraternity. It's doubtful that one ever appeared in a regular production car.

Seventy-one was to be another year of changes for Corvette, and they were painful ones to many observers. One event which greatly affected the Corvette was Chevrolet's move to de-proliferate its lineup, not just on the Corvette but with all its products. By 1970, there were literally hundreds of ways to order a Corvette between engine, trans-

1970, favorite of many, brought eggcrate grilles, the 454 and LT-1, and more standard equipment than ever before.

mission, and option package combinations. Chevrolet found this costly and, to a large degree, unnecessary. In the years to come, options – particularly *engine* options – would be de-proliferated out of the lineup.

WASHINGTON POWER BASE

Also making themselves felt throughout the early '70s were painful government regulations concerning emissions and safety standards. More than any real changes in hardware for '71, Ed Cole – by then president of GM – decreed that all cars should be capable of running on regular-grade 91 octane gasoline. Previously, they'd required premium-grade fuels as high as 103 octane. Cole, an astute engineer and administrator, correctly predicted that catalytic converters would soon be mandatory on all cars sold in America.

These converters couldn't handle lead additives, and without these additives, Cole knew, the octane ratings of readily-available pump gas would plummet.

To accept such low-octane fuel, compression ratios had to be reduced across the board. With this sudden crisis to be dealt with, little else could be done to the Corvette. 1971 models were virtually identical to those of 1970 except where options, engines, or power had been taken away.

Let's take some time, now, to discuss an event important to understanding all Corvettes of the 1970s. Beginning in 1972, American engines were rated in *net*, rather than *gross*, horsepower. Gross ratings represent an engine's power when hooked directly to a dyno. Net figures, meanwhile, measure the power that actually reaches the rear wheels. Accessory losses (driving the alternator, water pump, power steering pump, etc.), emissions equipment, and driveline losses are all figured into net ratings, so they're quite a bit lower than gross figures.

To illustrate, the 1972 LT-1 had 255 *net* bhp, but 310 *gross* bhp – same engine, same performance, but the power is rated by two different systems. Conversely, today's 385-horse (measured in *net* bhp) LT-5 is quite a bit stronger than the vaunted 435 (gross) bhp L71 of 20 years ago. See how it works? Now, how about why the industry did it?

The AMA went to net ratings to once again get out from under the critical gaze of Washington, D.C. Unlike the '57 racing ban, though, it didn't do much good. The switch also made following the declining engine outputs of the 1970s rather confusing, which may have been part of the plan as well.

Regardless of their rating system, just three Corvette engines were offered for 1972. Their net horsepower figures were 200 bhp for the base engine, 255 for the LT-1, and 270 for the LS-5, the last

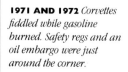

1971 AND 1972 *Corvettes fiddled while gasoline burned. Safety regs and an oil embargo were just around the corner.*

remaining big-block. The LS-5 wasn't offered in California, a victim of that state's much tighter emissions regulations.

By the way, there was one more change that made 1972 an important year in Corvette history: After 35 years, GM Styling changed its name. It's been known since May of '72 as GM Design Staff.

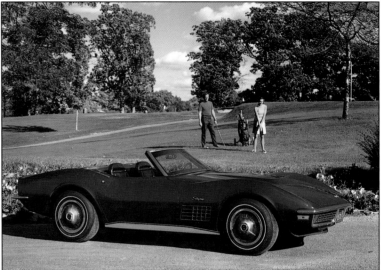

CIVILIZED BEHAVIOR

Nineteen seventy-three saw the first major changes to the Corvette body since 1970. Most noticeable was its new nose, a flexible, body-colored snout designed to meet the government's new regulations on impact resistance. One of these regs called for cars to withstand a 5 mph head-on collision without visible bumper or lighting damage. By passing impact energy through the rubber skin to two large deformable bolts, the Corvette met this goal handily. Ironically enough, the government-mandated nose also looked fantastic, harking back to the body-color

front end of the Mako Shark II. Seventy-three was the only year in which Corvettes had the slick new nose and the brutish old-style rear spoiler. It's earned a special collectability for the combination.

It was a year of refinement for the Corvette. Its body was attached to rubber bushings rather than the solid mounts used before, which resulted in fewer rattles and made the car seem tighter.

Speaking of rubber, a new type appeared on the car's wheels in 1973. Radial tires became standard, replacing the bias-plies of years past. While the radials lowered overall cornering grip, they were considerably quieter and smoother over the road. They also

ABOVE LEFT AND ABOVE RIGHT *1972, a year of change, was the last for chrome front bumpers and the first of net power ratings.*

BELOW LEFT *1973's federally mandated front bumper looked great, but the aluminum wheels were put off until 1976.*

improved the Corvette's wet-road behavior dramatically, an area of complaint from many owners. Heavier mats, undercoating, and insulation combined with the radials and rubber body mounts to make the '73 quieter and more civilized than any previous Corvette.

The 1970–1972 eggcrate side vents were replaced by functional single-scoop air extractors, and aluminum wheels were offered for the first time with the new bodystyle. Unfortunately, manufacturing problems kept the lightweight wheels from ever appearing on a showroom-bound car. The few '73s that got them were early publicity cars, or private cars retrofitted from supplies already shipped to dealers' parts departments.

Not surprisingly, power dropped once again as the grip of emissions laws tightened ever further. The base L48 engine made 190 net bhp, the L82

TOP RIGHT *Pop-off T-roof panels, a nice compromise between coupe and convertible, were a Corvette mainstay for 14 years.*

BELOW *It wasn't all regs and fuel costs in '73: Chevy's 4-rotor experimental was often touted as the Corvette of the future.*

BOTTOM *The combination of old tail, new nose, and "sugar scoop" side vents made for an attractive and unique 1973 model.*

small-block 250 bhp, and the LS4 454 came in at 275 net horses. Even with the base engine, however, Corvettes could still leap from 0–60 in less than seven seconds.

While the tire-smokers of the late '60s lamented the demise of their earthshaking engines, other buyers were finding out that they liked this new type of Corvette. It was quiet, agreeable, smooth, and handled like a dream. Though still plenty fast, it had cast off the rough edges, rattles, high-temperatures (both inside and out), and excessive thirst of a few years earlier.

Corvettes moved once again from the drag racer's market toward the quieter, more affluent buyers it was originally intended for. Increased sales of power steering, brakes, and automatic transmissions underscored the fact that once again buyers knew what the Corvette was all about. Women, too, were quickly becoming a large portion of the Corvette's market, something that would have surprised Harley Earl and Ed Cole in the early 1950s.

The bottom line was that they *sold*. By 1974, Corvette sales were beyond those of all but the

artificially lengthened 1969 model year. Seventy-four saw the completion of the change to body-colored, impact-absorbing bumpers. A rounded rear end – split vertically for this year only – appeared, and was at first rather controversial. Many people favored the more masculine tail of the earlier cars, but the new look was wholly in keeping with the Corvette's modern image.

It would be the last year of leaded fuel; catalytic converters came on line in 1975. Not coincidentally, 1974 was also the last year for the big-block engine. The 454 was by then emasculated to just 275 net bhp – a mere 30 horses more the '74 L82 small-block – and its acceleration was only marginally better than its lighter brother's. The big-block's cost in weight, handling, and mileage was too high for most buyers to bear. Fewer than 10% of the 37,502 Corvettes built that year had Mark IV power.

The last straw for the big-block was its failure to pass the government's tighter emissions tests for 1975. Time and money could have brought the engine into compliance, but Chevrolet correctly reasoned that in the midst of America's fuel crisis it was better to let the big-block die with dignity.

CORVETTE'S SWITCH *to impact-absorbing bumpers was completed in 1974. The vertical split in the rear bumper disappeared the following year.*

OIL CRISIS REFINEMENT

1975 brought a new type of Corvette to America. No, it looked just like the '74, except for some minor trim changes. But it was built for a world of costly fuel and increased safety concerns – its personality was that of a quick, responsible machine, rather than the rowdy hooligan it had been in recent memory. The heady days of cheap gas and a disorganized safety lobby were over. The Corvette was changing for the times. Output dropped again, this time to just 165 bhp for the L48, 205 bhp for the L84. Even considering that these were net figures, it

RIGHT *Trading brute strength for comfort, safety, and sophistication in 1975, sales climbed once more.*

BELOW *Reynolds Aluminium teamed with GM to build a lightweight version of the mid-engined XP-895. The girl was not included as standard.*

was the lowest output 2-engine lineup since 1955. It would be, in fact, the very lowest to which the Corvette's power levels would sink. By 1976, Detroit had gotten a grip on the realities of modern motoring and horsepower began to slowly rise back up.

Despite all this, the 1975 Corvette had plenty to recommend it. The interior had been upgraded constantly since '68, to the point that it was extraordinarily quiet and comfortable. The car felt light and willing, thanks to well calibrated power accessories, and it got respectable fuel mileage with or without the new 2.73 rear axle option.

An explosion-proof rubber bladder was hidden inside the fuel tank which made a fuel fire almost impossible. Front and rear bumper designs were changed to be even sturdier. Where the 1973 and 1974 used rubber over metal supports and deformable bolts, the 1975 had an all-new impact system of hydraulic dampers. Rather than deforming anything, the bumpers just bounced back.

Both the Corvette's price and 0–60 times climbed. A reasonably optioned car now easily passed the $7000 mark, and 0–60s were back up to the high 7-second range. There was, of course, still nothing on the road that could touch the Corvette's combination of price and performance. But the figures weren't nearly as staggering as they'd been a few years before.

Another victim of the mid-'70s drive toward responsible motoring was the Corvette convertible. 1975 would be its last year – or so it was believed. The convertible revival of the '80s was completely

← SKYRIDE

ABOVE AND LEFT *1975 marked a turning point for Corvette. In a relatively short time it had come to terms with modern demands.*

unexpected during the fuel- and safety-conscious days of 1975. Convertibles seemed profligate and frivolous to the public, and sales suffered accordingly. By 1975 just 12% of the near-record 38,465 Corvettes produced had open tops. At those figures, it wasn't worth Chevrolet's effort and expense to keep producing convertibles. The 1974 and 1975 convertible were some of the best-looking Corvettes of all time, but they were expected to be the end of the ragtop line.

One more change made 1975 a significant year for Corvette. On January 1, 1975 Zora Arkus-Duntov officially retired from Chevrolet. The man who'd coaxed, guided, and nurtured the Corvette – and the GM brass who controlled its fate – for more than 20 years, was going into retirement.

David R. McLellan took his place. McLellan's boyish looks betrayed little of his extensive experience in automotive engineering, testing, and design. Zora's departure left a fantastic void, and many people doubted that anyone so youthful in appearance and outlook could take his place. Dave McLellan would prove them wrong.

DAVID McLELLAN:
SILVER ANNIVERSARY

One of the first things buyers noticed about the 1976 car – the first "McLellan" Corvette – was that horsepower rates had climbed again. It as an admittedly small jump: five bhp for the L82, giving it a total of 210 horsepower, but at least it was a ray of hope for the future.

The aluminum wheels that were cancelled in '73 finally came on line in '76, giving the car a much-appreciated modern touch. A snappier torque converter helped 0–60 times drop below seven seconds

EVER-INCREASING
*sophistication was matched
by a resurgence in power
levels in McLellan's first
Corvette, the 1976.*

1976

again, and Corvette sales soared to more than 46,500 units. The next year, 1977, saw a minor interior re-design – though the gauges remained in the same layout, a new central console gave the interior a fresher, high-tech appearance.

The 1977 model also set new standards for fast, safe, and rewarding handling. Its overall grip was good, but its transition and response were without equal. ROAD & TRACK set a new slalom speed record for their magazine with a 1977 L82, besting the runner-up 911 Turbo Carrera by almost one mph. Luxurious leather seats became standard equipment that same year, as did power brakes and steering, but the base price climbed by more than $1000 to nearly $8700. Despite this unprecedented jump, production ran just shy of the magic 50,000 mark.

But it was the 1978 model that would really show McLellan's stuff. 1978 marked the 25th anniversary of the Corvette, and everyone knew that a major celebration was called for. Big plans were in the works to commemorate this milestone for Chevy's favorite son.

The most obvious addition to the now-10-year-old Corvette body was a sleek glass fastback, im-proving both aerodynamics and interior room con-siderably. The bubbleback added space for T-tops, grocery bags, luggage, or a few fetally-curled friends on the daily lunch run. Originally planned as a true hatchback with opening glass, a fixed rear window appeared on the production car. As with the '63–'68 coupes, fixed glass presented few real problems for the owners. When they wanted something from the back, they just reached, however ingloriously, over the seats.

McLellan and Chevrolet also squeezed a little more power from the venerable 350 small-block, five extra horses for the L48 and 10 more for the L82. Larger exhaust tracts did the trick, and the L82 received a new intake system as well. Unfortunately, no L82s went on sale that year in emissions-strict California.

Bringing the L82 up to 220 honest bhp meant that 0–60 times dropped once again to the mid-6-second range. Large, sticky Goodyear radials (255/70R-15), brought the Corvette's lateral acceleration to within a breath of the magic .80g mark at the same time.

While not posting quite the same slalom speeds as the 1977, the '78 Corvette cut an impressive figure over twisty roads.

The slower slalom times were probably the result of a shift in front/rear weight distribution from 49/51 to 46/54. This slightly upset overall balance, but the added rear traction was good news on slick pavement; in short, the monster Goodyears made the Corvette easier to drive fast than ever before.

Left-foot driving was the favorite pastime of L82 owners, but a new instrument panel and interior made plain old cruising a delight for all. The tachometer and speedo were removed from their individual pods and placed together in a single recessed box ahead of the driver. New door panels, cleaner and better finished than before, were added, and visibility through the new rear glass was superb. Finally, a pull-out screen allowed owners to hide their belongings in the car's rear.

In addition to all these mechanical advances, two semi-cosmetic option packages made the 1978 model year a collector's dream. The Silver Anniversary model featured a sophisticated two-tone paint scheme of light silver above dark silver; its interior

ABOVE LEFT *Kelsey-Hayes aluminum wheels appeared for good in 1976. Earlier versions were cancelled due to manufacturing woes.*

TOP AND ABOVE *When the fuel crunch put a Kaibosh on GM's rotary program the 4-rotor got a 400-inch V-8 and new name: Aerovette.*

LEFT *Fully aware of whose shoes he had to fill, David R. McLellan took over from Zora Arkus-Duntov on January 1, 1975.*

was treated to silver carpets, and mandatory aluminum wheels and sport mirrors came along for the ride. Silver Anniversary cars sold like mad, despite their $780 surcharge – $400 for paint, $340 for wheels, and $40 for mirrors.

The Silver Anniversary package wasn't cheap. Its price was chickenfeed, however, compared to the Limited Edition Corvette option – the so-called Pace Car. As they had with the 1969 Camaro, Chevrolet arranged to have a new Corvette pace the field for

the 1978 Indianapolis 500. A special commemorative edition was a must.

With base Corvettes selling for an already-hefty $9352, the Pace Car's $13,653 pricetag was a whopper. For that money, though, buyers got a bushel-basket of regular and special options thrown up. Most noticeable were the black and silver two-tone paint and unique spoilers. Also included were high-back bucket seats, power windows and door locks, air conditioning, tilt/telescope steering, aluminum

ABOVE *With optional FE7 gymkhana suspension, 1977 boasted stellar handling. Journalists found it exceptionally easy to drive fast.*

BELOW *The low, long Aerovette had drag numbers as good as its looks: .325 Cd; most cars were lucky to break .40.*

RIGHT *Perhaps out of respect for its elders, this 1978 shows great restraint in not smoking off its pristine 1953 rival.*

wheels, and much, much more. Chevrolet even included a set of owner-applied decals, reading *Official Pace Car*, for people who really wanted to stick out in traffic.

The company had originally planned to build just 1000 Pace Car replicas, but eventually made one for each dealer and change. In all, 6,502 Pace Cars were built, and uncounted '78s were converted to bogus Pace Car spec afterwards. Dealers were asking, and receiving, prices far above invoice for the black-and-silver specials, and a number of unscrupulous private owners wanted a share of the profits.

After such a big blowout, the 1979 models were understandably similar to the 1978s. Another five horses came to the L82, and 10 more were offered with the L48. Spoilers, basically the same as those on the '78 Pace Car, were also offered for $265. Installed, they decreased drag by about 15%.

MOVING UPMARKET

By 1980, the Corvette was undeniably showing its age. But it was definitely showing a timelessness as well. Still one of the best sports car bargains – one of

ABOVE *Designers originally conceived the aerodynamic 1978 backlight as an opening hatch; production models got fixed glass.*

LEFT *Two-tone Silver Anniversary option package made for one of the best-looking and most collectible Corvettes to date.*

OPPOSITE PAGE, TOP AND CENTER *The unique Pace Car replica appeared for 1978, as did 25th Anniversary badging.*

LEFT *Early publicity still shows the '79 with chrome trim around the rear window, but later cars used matte black in its place.*

BELOW AND OPPOSITE, BELOW *The L-82 V-8 picked up another five horses (for a 225 total) in 1979, while its L-48 brother received ten.*

the best sports cars, period – on the market, it continued to attract an ever-growing following.

But Chevrolet knew that the once-radical shape had become all too familiar to a world that had seen the Mazda RX-7, Porsche 928, Ferrari 308, and Datsun Z-Cars appear in the '70s. In response, McLellan's Corvette group was well on its way to designing an all-new machine for 1983. Until then, however, they were determined to keep the Corvette as current and competitive as it had always been.

Their answer to the newer competition came in the form of some truly modern upgrades. The 1980 Corvette was about 250 pounds trimmer than the 1979, through the use of lighter bumper assemblies, thinner door and windshield materials, a combined differential housing/crossmember made of aluminum, and an aluminum intake manifold for the L48. These and other measures improved acceleration, handling, and fuel economy.

Though still a young science in Detroit, a lot of thought was given to the car's aerodynamic drag. The Corvette's Cd (coefficient of drag) was dropped 12% below the already slippery Pace Car's figures with redesigned front and rear end caps.

Also arriving on the scene in the early '80s were CAFE (Corporate Average Fuel Economy) ratings, a system by which the government dealt fines to cars and companies with poor gas mileage. GM swore that they wouldn't let a single car fall to a CAFE "gas-guzzler" tax, and a fuel-sipping 3.07:1 rear axle became mandatory for the Corvette.

California buyers felt the hand of the government in a different, even heavier way. Chevrolet declined to certify the 350-cid engine for California's new and highly restrictive emissions regulations. Instead, they outfitted Corvettes headed for that state with the 305 cid V-8, an engine already California-certified ("Californicated") for the Camaro. Fitted with tubular

stainless steel headers the 305 still produced a re-spectable 180 bhp, but to some it seemed an ominous sign. Exactly 3221 305-equipped Corvettes were built, a considerably smaller percentage of production than California traditionally absorbed. It can only be assumed that a lot of people headed across state lines to purchase their new Corvette.

Despite their aggressive new looks and lightweight bodies, Corvette production was off by more than 20% for 1980. More than 53,800 1979s had been made: 1980 production settled in just above a less impressive 40,000.

1981 Corvettes carried an essentially unchanged exterior, but differences abounded elsewhere. The first thing people noticed was the L81, a new engine, and the removal of the long-standing L48 and L82. Much to the relief of the doom merchants, the Cali-fornia 305 was gone as well. In its place, though, was something perhaps even *more* ominous: a single, 50-state engine with 190 bhp. The 350-cid L81 eliminated the cost of producing three separate engines for the Corvette, but it put an end to higher output cars for those willing to pay the price.

Fortunately, the mandatory L81 was a fine engine. With magnesium rocker covers and stainless-steel

exhausts, it promised to make good on GM's pro-mise of healthy power and mileage through techno-logy. Computer Command Control, Chevrolet's name for their black-box electronic control module (ECM), handled the engine's emissions settings, timing, and intake mixture. The ECM adjusted these variables 10 times a second, according to inputs from sensors at the intake, exhaust, transmission, and elsewhere.

OPPOSITE PAGE AND ABOVE *By the end of the decade, Corvettes like this modified '78 were once again hunting on European soil.*

BELOW *The deep, aerodynamic chin of 1980-1982 models was functional as well as attractive. A matching deck spoiler graced the rear.*

ABOVE *1980s technology came on board in 1981 with computers, a fiberglass monoleaf rear spring, and stainless exhaust manifolds.*

Another high-tech feature of the '81 Corvette was its GRP (fiberglass) rear spring, which came on all cars with automatic transmissions and the standard suspension. At a mere eight pounds compared to the steel spring's 44 it would soon be available across the board.

By 1981, the base Corvette cost more than $16,250. This was still considerably less than anything in its performance league, but quite a bit more than the new breed of sports cars like RX-7 and 280ZX.

ABOVE *With a full 350 back under the hood, California Corvette drivers took to the hills again in 1981.*

Corvette's march upmarket was in many ways deliberate. Since Chevrolet had long been able to out-sell their production capacity with the car, prices and equipment standards had risen steadily.

Part of the increasing cost of Corvettes, however, was the result of outdated manufacturing equipment at the St. Louis assembly plant. St. Louis had been making the car in the same plant since 1954, and Chevrolet was ready to switch to a new, highly automated Corvette assembly facility in

Bowling Green, Kentucky. On June 1, 1981, Bowling Green took over production. St. Louis built cars simultaneously until August 1, then ceased Corvette production. Missouri's loss would be the Corvette lover's gain: Bowling Green's advanced facilities were, and are, ideally suited to the high-technology assembly required of today's Corvettes.

There were remarkably few teething woes with the new plant, and most buyers were unaware that such a major manufacturing change had taken place. Part of the easy transition can be attributed to GM's attempts to attract as many former St. Louis employees to Bowling Green as possible. Almost all of the line workers at Bowling Green had moved the 300 miles from St. Louis to take up their old jobs at the new factory.

Though they had to pay their own moving costs, the company helped with just about everything else. They offered assistance in finding housing and health care, provided social services, and opened large parts of the plant for community tours and meetings. As we'll see in the next chapter, Bowling Green became a model facility, both in working conditions and product quality.

LAST OF ITS KIND

It was no secret, even in the very early '80s, that an all-new Corvette was waiting in the wings. That 1982 would be the swan-song of the Mitchell/Shinoda bodystyle and the Cole/Duntov underpinnings was a well-known fact.

It was good news, to be sure; in the auto business, progress always is. But there were definitely those

1982 CORVETTES, *all built in the new high-tech plant at Bowling Green, Kentucky, featured TBI Cross Fire Injection.*

who would miss "the old girl," as the Corvette became known, and Chevy decided to make 1982 a fitting send-off for the platform that had served them so well for so long. Part of that send-off would be to give the car a healthy taste of the all-new model to come.

The year-old L81 gave way to the L83, a throttle-body-injected (TBI) 350 with 200 bhp. Its Cross Fire Injection system had nothing in common with the old Rochester constant-flow FI of 1957–1965.

Essentially, Cross Fire Injection used two electronic throttle bodies, one near each rocker cover, to squirt fuel directly into a single-plane aluminum intake manifold. From there the fuel/air mixture traveled through tuned intake runners to ports on the opposite side of the engine. The left-hand injector fed the right-hand cylinder bank and vice-versa; hence the name Cross Fire.

The ECM that made 10 decisions a second in 1981 was made capable of 80 adjustments a second with the TBI engine. Because of this new-found precision over timing and mixture, compression could be bumped from 8.2:1 to 9.0:1.

A new 4-speed automatic overdrive transmission became the only gearbox available, a high-tech job called the THM 700-R4. Having four gears, the top three with positive lockup, meant that 1st could be lower than before while 4th could be higher. Low and high gear ratios on the previous 3-speed auto-

DELICATE PAINT, *badging, and wheels set off the highly coveted Collector Edition.*

matic had been 2.52:1 and 1.00:1, respectively. On the 4-speed, they became 3.06:1 and 0.70:1.

The new powertrain was mandatory on all 1982s, but not all '82s were alike. At $22,538, the 1982 Collector Edition Corvette was the most expensive car Chevrolet had ever offered. It was also one of the most sophisticated and subtly attractive.

The Collector Edition's unique silver-grey metallic paint was set off by graduated gray decals on the hood and flanks. Delicately finished cloisonne medals graced the wheel centers and end caps. Aluminum wheels similar to those on the '63–'67 Corvette appeared, as did a luxurious leather and deep-pile carpet interior. Transparent T-top panels with a subtle bronze tint were unique to the car, and the Collector Edition was also the only Corvette of its generation to get a lift-up rear hatch.

All in all, the 1982 Corvette was widely appreciated as the last of a wonderful series of cars. It was the final expression of an inimitable character: a big, solid, fast, sports car that could be tame as a kitten in town but downright ferocious on the open road.

It was with great anticipation that the world looked forward to the next model – the first all-new Corvette in 20 years. But it was also with a bit of nostalgia and remorse. Since 1963, the Corvette had supplied the world with its own unique brand of fun and magic – no matter how good the next generation would be, they'd never build them the same way again.

ONLY THE COLLECTOR
Edition got an opening hatch in the old-style body. That and its unique detailing make it a rare find.

CHAPTER SIX

THE CURRENT GENERATION

ABOVE *The current Corvette won hearts and minds from the start, despite early expectations of a smaller, mid-engined design.*

When news began leaking out about the 1983 Corvette, many people asked the same question: why not a mid-engine? Enthusiasts had been expecting the next-generation Corvette to put its engine out back since the mid-engined Astro II showcar of 1968.

NO MIDDLE WAY

Originally that's how Chevy saw it, too. Surprisingly, the most ardent supporters of the mid-engine concept weren't GM engineers; they were members of Design Staff. They knew that a mid-engined car would give them a world of new shapes to work with. The idea of doing a rakish, forward-swept, racing-style car was exciting beyond words.

Management, too, was charmed by the mid-engine concept. The glamor of adopting the same layout as Ferrari and Lamborghini couldn't be denied.

But Dave McLellan wasn't willing to make such a major decision simply on the basis of what people expected. Would a mid-engine layout really help the Corvette's handling? Or, as he later demonstrated, would it simply make it inconvenient to own?

Beyond the image value of a mid-engine design, there turned out to be few advantages. The *theore-*

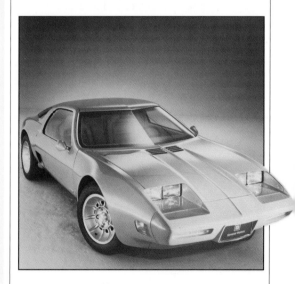

tical handling benefits of a mid-engine car are well established. These primarily concern the car's polar moment of inertia – that's just a fancy term to describe how close to the car's center most of its weight is. The more you concentrate the mass toward the middle, the more quickly the car should be able to change direction.

LEFT *Pontiac's Fiero became much of what Corvette might have been with the midship X-car V-6. Production ceased in 1988.*

BELOW *The X-car's V-6 ran fine, but wasn't strong enough for a Corvette. Later Fieros might have dropped it for the Quad-4.*

Racing cars take good advantage of this, but they don't have the air conditioner, bumpers, spare tire, power accessories, battery, and so on that today's street cars must carry. McLellan's engineers had to find room for all these, to say nothing of passengers. The handling benefits of a midship engine essentially evaporated after Chevy factored in the rest of the equipment that had to be spread around the car. Not surprisingly, the passengers would also be left with considerably less room inside.

There was also the problem of powering a mid-engined car. When work began on the new generation in 1977, America was still stinging from the OPEC oil embargo. Looming on the horizon were safety regulations, CAFE mpg quotas, and the spectre of $4/gallon gas. Doomsters were predicting the demise of the V-8 engine, and they had a lot of believers at GM. (If they could have seen the 385-bhp ZR1 back then they'd have passed out cold.)

It was very possible that the new Corvette would have a V-6, and if so a midship engine would have made more sense. GM was developing the front-wheel-drive X-Cars at the time, and the drivetrain could easily be adapted for mid-engine use – as Pontiac later showed with the Fiero.

Because the V-6 was so compact, many of the problems of a mid-engined V-8 were alleviated. Overall packaging, crash safety, and tire choices would be easier, though the engine and transmission

would need considerable redesigning to make and survive Corvette power levels.

Finally, GM decided that upcoming CAFE specs could be met by a high-tech small-block in a light-weight sports car package. And if the Corvette *could* come with a V-8, then it was universally accepted that it *should* come with a V-8. A Corvette without eight cylinders would be like Ronald Reagan without hair oil.

With that decision made, the mid-engine concept was washed up. There was no room, no transaxle and, according to Dave McLellan, just no good reason for the V-8 to be out back.

When the new car's layout was finally established, work could begin in earnest. The target was simple:

FAR LEFT Mid-engine prototypes like the 2-rotor XP-987GT teased Corvette lovers for years before the '84 appeared.

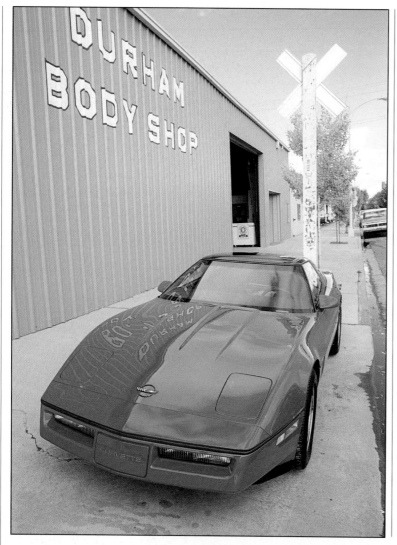

GM wanted the best-handling car in the world. It would have better cornering, better transient response, and better road feel than any other production vehicle on the planet. It would also be roomy, civilized, and reasonably priced.

The finished car hit the bullseye.

GETTING IT RIGHT

The secret of the current Corvette's superb handling lies in the successful integration of a number of advanced ideas. These begin right where the car touches the ground on massive Goodyears and don't stop until the peak of the basket-handle rollbar.

Unit-body construction techniques are used to build a central steel birdcage, totally unlike the previous car's ladder frame. Since the fiberglass skins are unstressed, the birdcage isn't a true unibody; it just uses the same method of building a structure from welded steel stampings.

The steel pieces, some of mild steel and others made from HSLA (High Strength Low Alloy), are fully galvanized for rust resistance. A special process had to be developed to weld the dissimilar metals.

Engineers drew up a basic design for the birdcage, then used computer testing and analysis to determine the final form. Since no crossmembers were used – they would have prevented the low height McLellan wanted – getting just the right tolerances everywhere was critical.

ABOVE *GM Design's simple yet swoopy skin managed to hide the plethora of high-tech goodies Engineering put inside.*

RIGHT *Extensive computer analysis and modeling helped engineers determine the exact design of the super-rigid HSLA birdcage.*

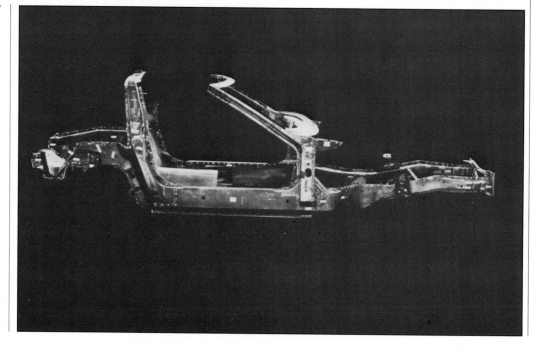

LEFT *This central chassis/ drivetrain/suspension package, attached from below during assembly, added tremendous stiffness.*

BELOW *As a V-6 looked likely for the next Corvette, GM built and tested this and other turbocharged prototypes.*

The design the team evolved remains with us today. The entire running gear – suspension, drivetrain, exhaust, and so on – is assembled as a separate unit and then attached to the birdcage during production. These pieces come in from the bottom, in part to avoid damaging the body panels which are already in place.

Aluminum suspension components are specified for their low unsprung weight and longevity. These are forged, rather than cast, for improved ductility. SLA (short/long arm) suspension up front was specified from the beginning, and a single-trailing-arm suspension was first tried at the rear. The rear suspension eventually settled on was a dual-trailing-arm design, however – again making use of forged aluminum components.

Springing for the new car took Duntov's transverse-leaf idea one step further: monoleaf fiberglass transverse springs appeared at both ends. The fiberglass springs weighed just 30% of what a conventional steel leaf would, they sagged less, and lasted longer. Bending forces within the spring also gave considerable anti-roll characteristics to the suspension, allowing smaller anti-roll bars.

The GRP springs were one of the most important elements of the new Corvette. They helped the car achieve the lowest body roll angles of any production vehicle while still allowing a smooth ride. They

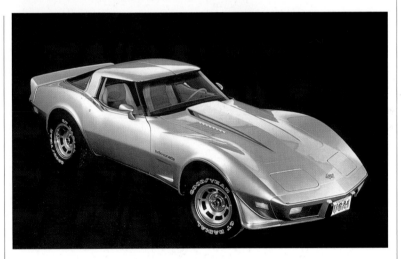

were also useful in tuning the car's handling: by changing the leaf's thickness, taper, or mounting points, more or less anti-roll and rebound could be dialed in with a minimum of fuss.

Goodyear and Chevrolet worked hand in hand to develop the Corvette's steamroller-sized Eagle GT tires and the result was rubber that exactly fitted the car's needs. As successive suspension changes were made to Corvette prototypes, Goodyear made prototype tires to match in kind. It was a stair-stepping process that yielded the best lateral acceleration numbers in production-car history – a full 1.01-g with unshaven tires and minor suspension adjustments. In production form, a still-record .90g was available. Cars like the Mustang were lucky to turn .75g at the time.

Since it yielded such phenomenal results, few people realize how long and trying the Corvette's handling program was. The first prototypes had a lot of trouble with flex-induced vibrations. As the frame became stiffer and stronger, the handling and overall feel of the car got better. But just when the package seemed to be coming together, a decision was made that would send it right back to square one.

GM originally intended to make the new Corvette a T-top as the previous generation had been.

TURBO EXPERIMENTALS *yielded indispensible data for both forced- and normally-aspirated engines.*

Management came to feel, however, that the Corvette should have a more exotic full targa roof.

In a targa, there's no T-bar to tie the windshield to the rear basket handle. Now that T-bar may look a little odd, but it provides a great deal of stiffness to a car's structure. When the word came down to lose the T, the engineers had to go back and find even more rigidity from the birdcage – and at first it didn't seem possible. Strange vibrations cropped up, and the development cars threw fits. But Fred Schaafsma, a handling wizard fresh from the successful '82 Firebird/Camaro program, came aboard to help iron out the problems. His suggestions formed the basis for the final, highly successful birdcage the car would eventually use. Building a superb suspension system into the car was only possible after the basic structure was set up correctly.

The TBI V-8 and THM 400-R4 transmission from the 1982 Corvette were carried over into the new car. There was, however, to be a manual transmission offered – the Doug Nash T-10 4-speed. The Doug Nash T-10 was basically an upgraded version of the old Borg-Warner 4-speed that served with distinction in 1957–1966 Corvettes. It had come on line again in 1978–1981.

Nineteen eighty-three's CAFE quotas meant that some sort of overdrive would be needed. After looking into an old Warner design and the European GKN/Laycock overdrive, GM settled on a unit Doug Nash was developing for off-road use. Bolted in unit with the ex-Warner 4-speed, the drivetrain was capable of seven forward speeds – overdrive was available in all but first gear.

As always, the Corvette's body came out of a design effort no less monumental than Engineering's. When Jerry Palmer, then the chief designer for the Corvette, first began working on the new car in 1977 he wanted a midship engine. As we know, however, that's not what he got. What Palmer and the men of Chevy Three (the studio now responsible for Corvette design) evolved instead was a sleek, low-slung coupe with lots of traditional Corvette influence.

The new body was more modern, more aerodynamically efficient, roomier inside, smaller outside, and easier to manufacture than the previous one. There were no bonding seams, thanks to the beltline groove added by young stylist John Cafaro. Bonding

ABOVE *Clamshell hood opens wide to reveal the fuel-injected V-8, serpentine belt system, and cast aluminum suspension pieces.*

seams occur where two pieces of fiberglass must be glued together to make a single finished panel. The seams had been notorious troublespots on the old Corvette: they'd warp, crack, and make lots of dust during sanding. A real pain during production, Chevy made a point of eliminating the seams early on.

Irv Rybicki, who replaced Bill Mitchell as head of GM Design Staff in 1977, and his eventual successor Chuck Jordan, were constantly heading over to Chevy Three to oversee Palmer and his crew. The two executives were instrumental in giving the Corvette its subtle, flowing fender lines. The Chevy Three designers had been working so closely with the car that outsiders Rybicki and Jordan could make suggestions the full-time stylists hadn't thought of.

"A STAR IS BORN"

The slick new body and chassis were mated together and fitted with all sorts of high-tech gear, including lightweight Girlock brakes, a full clamshell hood à la Mako Shark II, and a high-tech LCD instrument panel. In early 1983, the Corvette went into production.

1984 (above) and 1985 models had just one readily visible difference: subtle Tuned Port Injection badges on the beltline.

Most people will tell you that there were no 1983 Corvettes. They're wrong. True, when the first customer cars were shipped out in February of '83, Chevy had already decided to register and sell them as 1984 models. They wanted to have the first '84s on the market, rather than the last '83s.

But the first 43 cars – 10 prototypes and 33 pilot vehicles – were, in fact, assembled with 1983 build plates and VINs (Vehicle Identification Numbers).

Since none of these were ever sold to the public, they're often overlooked in Corvette lore. You can win a few bar bets with this one, though.

Production Corvettes #0002 through #0070 were built as test vehicles, though most of the later cars were eventually sold off. The serial number 0001 was reserved for the 71st Corvette built, which was donated to the National Council of Corvette Clubs' spina bifida charity raffle. The first customer-

plaints popped up. The top-of-the-line Z51 suspension was one trouble spot. It was, apparently, too much of what the magazines had asked for.

The base suspension and tires delivered more grip than most writers had ever encountered, yet the Z51 was stiffer and stickier still. Too much so, many felt. There was even an unsubstantiated rumor that went as far as saying the Z51 could crack the roof panel if the car went over a sharp bump.

Some writers also complained that the car was too heavy, being only about 250 pounds lighter than its predecessor. That its weight and performance compared admirably with the Porsche 928S, BMW 633, and Ferrari 308 was rarely mentioned. Other drivers, wanting a dramatic, heart-pounding confrontation with the new Corvette, were disappointed by the car's easy-going nature. It went *calmly* like a bat out of hell, without all the noise and chassis-jacking of the competition. Many drivers, apparently, didn't realize just how fast they were really going.

THE RAGTOP RETURNS

Much as with Corvettes past, the history of the car's current generation is one of subtle refinements for major results. In its first year it was good enough to be MOTOR TREND's Car of the Year. Annual upgrades ensured not only a constantly improved package but a yearly appearance as one of CAR & DRIVER's Ten Best Performers.

The first big changes came in '85, though you'd be hard-pressed to see them from the outside. Tuned Port Injection (TPI) came on line to replace the previous car's Cross Fire (TBI) system. With one injector at each intake port, rather than the TBI's two for the entire engine, port injection added 25 horsepower and 40 ft./lbs. of torque. ROAD & TRACK measured 0–60 times for the hopped-up 'Vette at 6.2 seconds and their quarter-mile sprint took just 8.2 seconds more. TPI also gave a whopping 11% boost in EPA-rated fuel mileage.

That same year, shock and spring rates were refined to smooth out the Z51's behavior on rough roads. Wider front tires – up an inch to a full 9.5 – improved overall handling despite the more civilized settings.

In 1986, Bosch ABS II anti-lock brakes were added to the package. Without getting into too much detail, the Bosch system would automatically

TPI *(Tuned Port Injection) appeared in '85, bringing 25 more horses and a more usable delivery curve to the venerable 350.*

bought car was #0071, the 70th car off the line. Cochran & Celli, an Oakland, California, Chevy dealer, sold it to Mr. Bob Nagy.

The media's reaction to the car was, in a word, ecstatic, though they'd been expecting a new car since '72 and crying out for a mid-engined model. Those two facts should have made the new car, no matter how good, a disappointment to many. It wasn't.

"A Star is Born," said MOTOR TREND. "Fantastic," was the word from ROAD & TRACK. "America takes on all comers," quoth CAR & DRIVER. Let loose for early previews in pilot cars and engineering specials, the country's auto journalists waxed poetic over the new Corvette's looks, handling and performance.

As the year progressed, production models trickled into the magazines' stables and a few com-

LEFT *TPI also gave owners a whopping 11% increase in fuel economy and another 40 foot-pounds of torque.*

BELOW *This was the most common view of the 1985 Corvette. The car was more than a match for machines three times the price.*

adjust brake fluid pressure to prevent panic-stop lockups. Accelerating to 60 mph in about six seconds, by '86 the Corvette could decelerate back to zero in less than 130 feet! The only other car with that sort of braking was Ferrari's BB512 Boxer. Lacking ABS, however, it took an expert driver to get the Boxer's braking distances down that low.

Eighty-six also saw the return of the long-rumored Corvette convertible. Introduced in mid-year, the trim ragtop sported a folding roof and, once again, aluminum cylinder heads. The lightweight aluminum heads were finally here to stay: they became standard as soon as production got up to speed.

Because the Corvette was already a full targa, surprisingly little additional bracing was required for the convertible conversion. Basically, a hefty X-brace was added beneath the passenger compartment and the K-braces at the cowl were beefed up.

CONVERTIBLES *like the 1986 Indy 500 Pace Car Replica (center left) should bring astronomical sums in the years ahead.*

ABOVE *Similar to the 1968-1975 convertible mechanism, the ragtop introduced in 1986 hid under a spring-loaded fiberglass panel.*

SINCE THE *super-stiff coupes were already full targas, convertibles needed very little extra structural bracing.*

Anyone familiar with the 1968–1975 Corvette droptop already knew how the current convertible top operates. A fiberglass panel at the rear of the passenger compartment hid the assembly in the down position. To put the top up, the driver opened the panel (electrically or with a manual override), attached the header rail to the windshield, put the panel back down, and pushed two guide pins into holes on the rear deck. Despite its simplicity, the padded top was remarkably snug when erected.

The 200-horse L83 of 1982 evolved – through cam and induction changes, roller lifters, compression-ratio jumps, and so on – into the 245 bhp L98 of 1988. With torque climbing to a lofty 330 ft./lbs., Chevy's official 0–60 time for the manually-shifted L98 dropped to 5.3 seconds.

That same year, Corvettes received new wheels, the first significant external change since '84. The Z51 package now offered 13-inch front discs (12-inchers were standard) and larger 17-inch wheels to clear the oversized rotors. The standard 16-inchers were redesigned in the bargain.

ABOVE *1988 brought optional 13-inch brake discs and 17-inch wheels to the race-bred Z51.*

RIGHT *Corvette seats, real leather and adjustable for everything short of blood types, were often hailed as the best in the business.*

TOP RIGHT *A GTO body kit, developed for racing but sold through Chevy dealers, was considered a legitimate Corvette option.*

ABOVE RIGHT AND RIGHT *White body-color wheels and a stand-out black roof pillar distinguished 1988 35th Anniversary model.*

AFTERMARKET WHEELS
*(above) were a favorite
addition, but production
items (center right) inspired
many imitators.*

RIGHT *Headlights rotated
on an axis perpendicular to
the driveline. Plenty of
headaches went into getting
them right.*

OPPOSITE *The fast and
elusive Western Mountain
Corvette, seen here in its
natural habitat, is far from
extinction.*

CALLAWAY

In October of 1986, auto enthusiasts received official confirmation of a rumor they'd long been hoping was true. Their favorite magazines let them know that Chevrolet, in a murkily defined relationship with Callaway Engineering of Old Lyme, Connecticut, would offer a 345-horse twin-turbo Corvette for sale to the public.

Chevy did their best to downplay their affiliation with Callaway, but there was little doubt that the companies were in full cahoots. Chevy even assigned the Callaway its own option number: RPO B2K made the twin-turbo an official Chevrolet, covered by the same type of warranties and dealer network that any other of their products enjoyed.

The $51,000 Callaway was the fastest car this side of the Ferrari Testarossa and GTO, both of which cost well over $110,000. It turned quarter miles in 13 seconds flat, 0–60s in about 4.5 seconds, and topped out just shy of 180 mph. More than one Corvette

ABOVE *Though missing the usual roof-pillar badging, the airy wheels and high top end of this Corvette spelled Callaway.*

BELOW *Fair warning to Ferrari and Porsche drivers, the LT5 emblem stood for big numbers: 4 cams, 385 bhp, 180+ mph.*

B2K headed off to the *Autobahn* to settle some old scores. By the time Callaway arrived, Chevy had been playing with twin-turbo 'Vettes for quite a while. At first these were V-6-powered experimentals, built toward the day when a V-6 Corvette might be necessary to meet CAFE quotas. Later, twin-turbo V-8s were built just to see how fast a Corvette could really go.

"Thumper," one of those force-fed V-8s, was seeing nearly 200 mph by the time the Callaway was born. Chevrolet could certainly have built a car like the Callaway on its own – were GM of a mind to allow it. But Reeves Callaway, the acknowledged leader in aftermarket turbos, was an easy way around management's worries.

Officially, Chevrolet never sold Callaways. They sold turbo-ready B2Ks to which Callaway added all the necessary hardware, and it was up to the dealer to purchase the car from there. GM didn't release material or advertising on the twin-turbos, and never mentioned them as products. They did, however, provide Callaway with engineering support, an RPO and warranty as mentioned, and specially-prepared B2K blocks.

ZR1: AMERICAN SUPERCAR

But the Callaway's status as the ultimate American car changed with the arrival of the next – and this time fully GM-blessed – super Corvette. Listen to this: 385 bhp, 180+ mph, six forward speeds, 30 mpg, $49,000, 4 cams, 32 valves, and 16 individual intake runners. Want one?

Well, all you had to do was go down to your local Chevy dealer and order up a Corvette with RPO ZR1. You'd find yourself in possession of the fastest, most advanced Corvette ever.

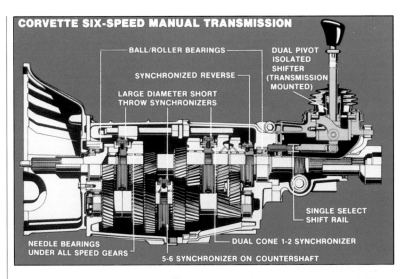

CORVETTE SIX-SPEED MANUAL TRANSMISSION

BALL/ROLLER BEARINGS

DUAL PIVOT ISOLATED SHIFTER (TRANSMISSION MOUNTED)

SYNCHRONIZED REVERSE

LARGE DIAMETER SHORT THROW SYNCHRONIZERS

SINGLE SELECT SHIFT RAIL

NEEDLE BEARINGS UNDER ALL SPEED GEARS

DUAL CONE 1-2 SYNCHRONIZER

5-6 SYNCHRONIZER ON COUNTERSHAFT

TOP LEFT *The six-speed ZF gearbox, introduced in 1989, marked a new high point in production car transmission technology.*

TOP RIGHT *Only subtle differences on the outside – rounded end cap, squared taillights, wider rear body – graced the 1989 ZR1.*

ABOVE *Giant rear tires were needed to get all that LT5 power to the ground, and a widened rear body appeared in turn to cover them.*

LEFT *Many journalists called the ZR1 the Heart Attack, not Heartbeat, of America.*

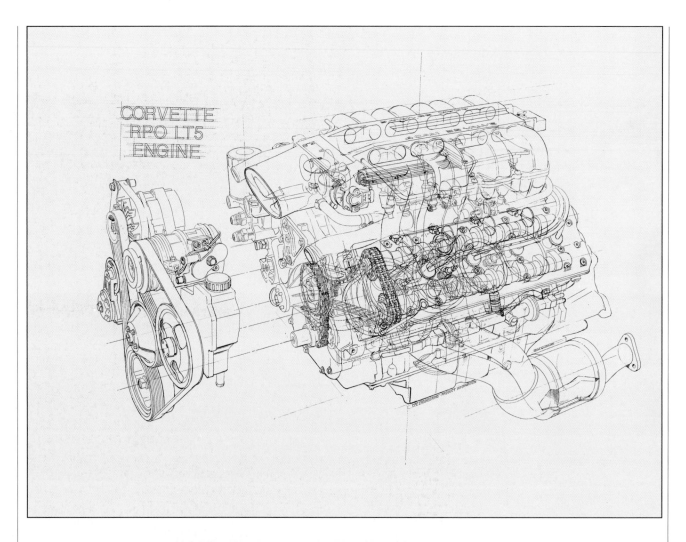

ABOVE *Ordered by Chevrolet, designed by Lotus, and built by Mercury Marine: a lot goes on inside the powerhouse LT5.*

RIGHT *Promised from the start of convertible production in '86, a sharp-looking hardtop finally appeared in '89.*

The ZRI's heart was the LT5 engine, an all-aluminum, normally aspirated quad-cam developed by Lotus, GM's newly acquired engineering division. What began as a program to put 4-valve heads on the L98 evolved into an all-new, super-high-tech engine. The LT5 shared just one component, the rear main bearing seal, with the regular 350 Chevy.

Chevrolet set down seemingly impossible targets for the 32-valve engine. It was to have more power than the big-blocks of days gone by, fit into the already snug Corvette engine bay without a hood scoop, and be more docile than the babydoll L98. And while you're at it, GM told Lotus, give it better mileage than the L98, too.

Amazingly, the LT5 fulfilled all those goals. It was actually two engines in one – two distinctly different intake and valve packages were included in the single powerplant. Each cylinder had two intake and two exhausts valves, two port injectors, and two tuned intake runners. The primaries were for regular driving – the secondary pieces came into play for all-out performance.

The primary intake system was fed by a single .87-inch butterfly. This meted out air to the eight primary intake runners, which led to valves operated

TOP *Though the padded soft top did an excellent job, dealers sold hardtops individually to retrofit 1986 and later convertibles.*

There are very few differences in the skins of models produced between 1984 and 1989 (shown here). The convertible was first introduced in mid-1986.

by a set of mildly-ground lobes on the overhead camshaft.

This small-induction, low-overlap formula was good for low-end torque, driveability, and fuel efficiency. Running on just this primary circuit, the LT5 gave about the same performance as the L98.

Get into the gas, though, and the secondary intake system kicked in: two 2.32-inch throttle plates slapped open and oxygen poured into the remaining eight intake runners. Port injectors dumped fuel directly upstream of intake valves bumped by a second set of lobes, these ones with a radical, high-overlap grind. It was the secondary system that supplied the LT5's prodigious top-end power.

The ZR1 put that power to the ground through massive 315/35ZR-17 tires, the largest then offered in America. In plain talk, the tires were 315mm (12.4 inches) wide, mounted on 17-inch wheels, and rated for sustained speeds over 180 mph. The ZR1 carried all-new rear bodywork to cover the giant rubber, though only the square lamps in a slightly more rounded tail cap were an obvious tip-off to what lurked under the hood.

In addition, the ZR1 had a unique "valet" switch –

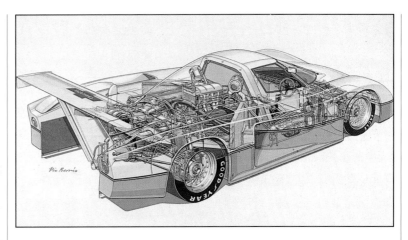

a key-controlled lockout for the heavy-duty butterflies and injectors. This allowed the ZR1 to be driven by valets, kids, mothers-in-law, and anyone else the regular driver didn't think was quite ready for 385 horses.

Despite all these things – and variable-damping shocks, a 6-speed ZF transmission it shared with all manual '89s, and more – the ZR1 went on sale for a couple of thousand dollars less than the B2K Callaway. Buyers could, in theory anyway, get change back from their $50,000.

AMA RACING BANS *having faded like a bad memory, Corvette GTP won twice in 1986 and set an IMSA record, capturing seven pole positions.*

ABOVE *1988 SCCA Trans-Am; winners at Mosport.*

RIGHT *1988 GTP.*

BELOW *Invincible in Showroom Stock, SCCA set Corvettes up in their own one-car series called Corvette Challenge.*

And oh yes, one more thing: with its super-wide rear tires, the ZR1 was not only the fastest Corvette to date, it was the best handling as well. It could pull 1.2g through corners – more than most racing cars.

Racing cars, by the way, seem once again to hold the future of the Corvette. After finally renouncing their compliance with the AMA racing ban, factory-assisted Corvettes and Corvette-based competition cars are once again winning races around the world. Led by names like Childress, Brassfield, Protofab, and Peerless, silhouette and prototype Corvettes are the terror of American road racing. There are IMSA GTO and GTP Corvettes, SCCA Trans-Am entries, drag racers, and more.

Showroom Stock racing was particularly kind to the current Corvette. For three years straight Corvettes won every single race in SCCA's Escort Endurance Series for Showroom Stock Automobiles – the string was only broken by SCCA giving up, outlawing the car and starting up a new series for Corvettes alone. The Corvette Challenge became one of America's most exciting and hotly-contested racing series.

It's always dangerous to predict the future of America's only sports car, but the racetrack is as safe a place to look as any. Chevrolet's current look at the future is something called the Corvette Indy, an IMSA-like mid-engined coupe with 4-wheel-drive, 4-wheel-steering, and an LT5 engine. (It debuted with a streetable version of Chevy's Indy-winning CART V-8.)

Many people have been forced to eat their words two years after declaring a Chevy showcar as the Corvette of a few years down the road, and MOTOR TREND's vision of the Corvette Indy's future is almost certainly no exception. The Indy showcar is, however, proof positive that the Corvette will be with us for as long as there are people who love to drive. As for the true face of the next generation, well, we'll just have to wait and see what the future brings.

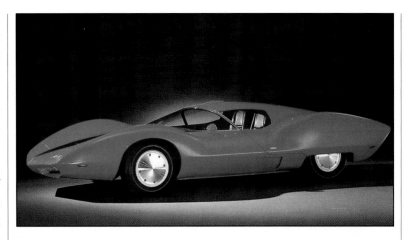

TOP TO BOTTOM *Past looks at the future; Astro I, Astro II (or XP-880), and Astro III, never hit showrooms. Who's to say what the next Corvette will look like?*

IN JANUARY *of 1986 Chevrolet introduced the most radical, forward-thinking Corvette prototype to date: the Corvette Indy. Developed in great part by Lotus, the Indy sported 4-wheel drive, 4-wheel steering, active suspension, CRT cockpit screens, and a transverse mid-ship version of the 2.67-liter Chevy racing engine that went on to dominate Indy competition.*

The racing engine was later replaced with an LT5, and in that form MOTOR TREND reported the possibility of a limited production run. Whether this look to the future would be any more accurate than most was a topic discussed for years.

SPOTTER'S GUIDE TO CORVETTES 1953-1989

ABOVE *Even from inside the cockpit, the thin, protruding fender line is a mark of single-headlight 1956 and 1957 Corvettes.*

1953–1955

Headlamps are recessed behind mesh screens, taillights protrude rearward. Body sides are flat. V-8 (1955) models have a large golden "V" in Chevrolet script behind front wheel.

1956–57

Single exposed headlight per fender thrusts forward and taillights are recessed into rear fenderline. Single grilled has 13 "teeth." Scooped-out side cove is unadorned. The fiberglass hardtop appears as an option.

1958–1960

Dual headlights on each fender have chrome bezels and are located above one central (9-tooth) grille and two outer intakes. Only the 1958 car has a louvered hood and two chrome spears on trunk.

1961–1962

Tail completely new with high beltline, flat trunk, and four taillights below crease. Headlights are painted body color and teeth are removed from grille and replaced by mesh. 1961 retains three chrome spears in cove and chrome cove surrounds. 1962 deletes cove surround and has a grille, not spears, for decoration.

1963–1964

New Sting Ray body of 1963 has high beltline crease, hidden headlights. 1963 has two horizontal simulated vents, one above the other, behind the front wheel and simulated mesh air extractors in the hood's lead-ing edge. 1963 coupe has the split-window bar across rear glass; many of these were later removed by owners. 1964 has no trim in the hood vent depressions, removes bar from rear window of coupe, and goes to finned air extractors on the coupe's B-pillars. (1963 used two dummy scoops.)

1965–67

1965–66 Sting Rays have three vertical louvers behind each front wheel and the hood depressions are gone entirely. 1965 grille has black-out paint on horizontal bars while the 1966 cars have an egg-crate grille pattern. 1967 car gets unique side vents – five slots in a box-shaped depression. Big-block '67s have a unique scoop-style hood bulge.

ABOVE *The big block hood scoop and gills-in-a-box side vents make this a 1967, but the body style dates from 1963.*

LEFT *GM Design's Mako Shark II grew up to be the 1968-1982 Stingray. Four-gill side vents appeared on 1968 and 1969 models.*

BELOW *Easily spotted by their eggcrate grilles and metal bumpers front and rear, 1970-1972 models were the last of a breed.*

1968–1969

New wasp-waist body is virtually identical between years, though the '69 features "Stingray" script above side louvers. ("Stingray" replaces "Sting Ray" this year.) 1969 cars have back-up lights in their taillight lenses – those of 1968 can be found under the rear bumper.

1970–72

Egg-crate side vents and grilles appear on all models and square exhaust exits are formed into the rear valance panel. 1970 through 1972 are virtually identical externally and are the last Corvettes with chrome bumpers front and back.

1973

The 1973 Corvette has a body-colored soft front bumper and the older-style chrome rear bumpers. Side louvers change to a single-opening, functioning design that remains until 1980.

1 – Fastback rear glass first appears: 1978.
2 First single-opening, functional side louvers: 1973.
3 All Collector Editions: 1982.
4 Round badging and usually aluminum wheels – though these are wearing stock steel units: 1976.
5 Widened rear body work, LT5 badges – ZR1: 1989.

1974–1977

Soft bumpers appear front and rear in 1974; 1975 brings vertical black pads on the front end and a one-piece rear section. (The 1974's rear bumper has a central vertical split.) 1976 cars are virtually identical to 1975s but the vents behind the rear window are gone. 1976 is also the first year for widespread use of Kelsey-Hayes aluminum wheels. 1977 sees the front emblem changed from a round badge to crossed flags, and the windshield pillars are thinner – a minute detail at best. Easier to spot is the change in alarm-switch locations. Earlier cars have a special lock switch on the front fender that's missing from most 1977s.

1978-79

Fastback rear glass appears in 1978. Unique circular 25th Anniversary emblems are used front and rear – all Pace Car and Silver Anniversary models are 1978 cars. 1979 goes to elongated crossed-flag emblems and blacked-out rear window trim.

1980-82

1980 and 1981 are virtually identical on the outside. Both years use aggressive new end caps with integral spoilers front and rear – the so-called "big chin" package. On close observation, the 1980 model has a silver rib across the rocker panel while the 1981's rocker is all black. 1982 uses unique Cross Fire Injection logo above side vent, and all Collector Edition models are 1982 cars.

1984-1989

The all-new Corvette debuts in 1983 as a 1984 model. 1985 cars get a Tuned Port Injection logo above their side vents. A convertible model is introduced in mid-1986, and new wheels grace all 1988 models. Except for colors and brake-light locations there's very little external difference between the '84–'89 models. Callaway twin-turbo gets two NACA ducts in the hood and special badges. The ZR1 has widened rear bodywork, a rounded rear end cap with squared-off taillights, and special LT5 badges.

CORVETTE PRODUCTION

In the beginning, all Corvettes were roadsters. It wasn't until 1963 that the coupe entered the lineup of America's favorite sports car. In all, 212,016 of the 816,958 Corvettes produced between 1953 and the end of the 1985 model year were topless models.

Here's a rundown of the year-by-year production numbers:

YEAR	ROADSTER	COUPE	TOTAL
1953	300		300
1954	3,640		3,640
1955	700		700
1956	3,467		3,467
1957	6,339		6,339
1958	9,168		9,168
1959	9,670		9,670
1960	10,261		10,261
1961	10,939		10,939
1962	14,531		14,531
1963	10,919	10,594	21,513
1964	13,925	8,304	22,229
1965	15,376	8,186	23,562
1966	17,762	9,958	27,720
1967	14,436	8,504	22,940
1968	18,630	9,936	28,566
1969	16,632	22,130	38,762
1970	6,648	10,668	17,316
1971	7,121	14,680	21,801
1972	6,508	20,496	27,004
1973	4,943	25,520	30,463
1974	5,472	32,029	37,501
1975	4,629	33,832	38,461
1976		46,558	46,558
1977		49,034	49,034
1978		46,772	46,772*
1979		49,901	49,901
1980		40,564	40,564
1981		40,593	40,593
1982		25,407	25,407**
1983		0	0
1984		51,547	51,547
1985		39,729	39,729
1986	7,264	27,673	34,937
1987	10,625	20,007	30,632
1988	7,315	27,794	35,109
Total:	**237,220**	**680,416**	**917,636**

* – Includes 6,501 Limited Edition models
** – Includes 6,759 Collector's Edition models

CORVETTE SUCCESS

Chevy's Corvette has enjoyed success in racing almost since the day it was introduced. Here are some highlights of its racing heritage:

1955 Set stock car record for Pike's Peak Hill Climb.

1956 Ran 150 mph on Daytona Beach, SCCA C-Production champion, 15th overall in Sebring 12-hour.

1957 First in class at Sebring, SCCA B-Production and B-Sports/racing champion.

1958 First in GT at Sebring, first in sports car division at Pike's Peak, SCCA B-Production champion.

1959 SCCA B-Production champion.

1960 First in class at Sebring, eighth overall at Le Mans 24-hour, SCCA C-Sports/Racing and B-Production champion.

1961 First in GT at Sebring, first in class at Pike's Peak, SCCA B-Production champion.

1962 First in class at Daytona Continental, SCCA A and B-Production champion.

1963 SCCA B-Production champion, first in Prototype class at Nassau.

1964 First in GT at Daytona Continental, SCCA B-Production champion.

1965 SCCA Midwest division A and B-Production champion, SCCA Southwest division B-Production champion.

1966 First in GT, Daytona Continental and Sebring.

1967 First in GT at Sebring, ran first in GT at Le Mans until engine failed.

1968 First in class at Sebring.

1969 SCCA A and B-Production champion.

1970 SCCA A and B-Production champion.

1971 First in GT (fourth overall) in Daytona 24-hour, first in GT at Sebring, SCCA A and B-Production champion.

1972 Running first in class at Le Mans until component failure, SCCA A and B-Production champion.

TOP *The long-nosed SR-2, 1956: part racer, part publicity chaser.*

ABOVE *Option Z06, 1962: competition spec Sting Ray.*

RIGHT *Owens-Corning, '69/70.*

1973 First in class at Sebring, SCCA B-Production, B-Stock Solo II and B-Prepared Solo II champion.

1974 SCCA A and B-Production champion, SCCA B-Stock Solo II champion.

1975 First overall SCCA Trans Am series, SCCA A-Production champion.

1976 SCCA A and B-Production and B-Stock Solo II champion.

1977 SCCA A-Production, B-Stock Solo II and B-Prepared Solo II champion.

1978 First overall in Trans Am Category II, SCCA A and B-Production, B-Stock Solo II, B-Prepared Solo II and B-Stock Ladies Solo II champion.

1979 First in Riverside Vintage Car Races (Grand Sport #003), first overall in Trans Am Category I, SCCA B-Production, B-Stock Solo II, B-Prepared Solo II and B-Stock Ladies Solo II champion.

1980 Second overall, SCCA Trans Am series.

1981 First and Third overall SCCA Trans Am series.

1982 Tied for second overall, SCCA Trans Am series.

1984 SCCA Trans Am win at Road Atlanta, SCCA Showroom stock endurance wins at Mid-Ohio and Willow Springs, SCCA showroom stock national champion.

1985 IMSA-GTO win at Laguna Seca, SCCA showroom stock endurance wins at Riverside, Sears Point, Road Atlanta, Nelson Ledges, St. Louis, Lime Rock and Mid-Ohio SCCA showroom stock manufacturer's champion. Corvette SSGT national champion, SCCA runoffs, Atlanta. IMSA-GTP Corvette on pole at Daytona with new lap record.

1986 Won all seven SCCA races. Corvette GTP won twice and also set an IMSA record, capturing seven pole positions.

1987 Won all SCCA races. Corvette GTP took four pole position. Corvette GTO had one pole position.

1988 IMSA GTO wins at Sebring and Lime Rock. SCCA Trans-Am win at Mosport. SCCA Corvette Challenge established.

INDEX

Page references in italics refer to illustrations.

A

acceleration 27, 37, 80, 81, 97, 102, 103, 105, *see also* performance
Aero Coupe *73*
aerodynamics 87, *89*
Aerovette *83, 84*
Alembic 19
aluminum 34, 38
AMA racing ban 38, *41*, 48, 51
Andrey, Gaston 28
anti-roll bars *34*
Arkus-Duntov, Zora, 7, 22-6, *23, 24*, 34, 40, 42-3, 48-51, 54, 56, 63, 71-3, 81
assembly plants, Bowling Green *16*, 91
Flint *15*, 16
St Louis *16*, 90-1
Astro *117*

B

Barr, Harry 19, 27
birdcage 96, *96*
Blue Flame Six 13
bodies 99, *114*
'68 72
fiberglass *14*, 15-16, 43, 96
GTO kit *107*
production 15–16
Scaglietti 38
Sting Ray 45, *46*
XP-720 54
body roll 34
bracing 103, *105*
brakes 13, 31, 32, 45
Bosch anti-lock 102-3
disc 40, 64
drum 42, 43, 65
power 65
Brock, Peter 45
bumpers 77, *77*, 79, 80

C

C-modified championship 48
Cafaro, John 99
CAFE ratings 87, 95
Callaway 110, *110*
camshaft 24
catalytic converters 75, 79
CERV *37*, 38

chromium 28, 31, 37
Cobras 51, *52*, 53, *61*, 61, *62*, 67
Cole, Edward N. 7, 11, 19, 25-7, 27, 43, 48, 56, 75
Collector Edition 92, *92, 93*
colors 30
consoles 30
convertibles 80-1, 103, *104*, 105
Corvair *16*, 18
Corvette Challenge *116*, 117, *125*
coupe *55*
coves 23, 30, 38
Cross Fire Injection 92
Cunningham, Briggs 35
Curtice, Harlow (Red) 44
Cutitta, Lou *40*, 44
cylinder heads, aluminum 103

D

Davis, Grady 51, 61
Daytona Beach *23*, 24
DeLorean, John 48, 74
Doane, Dick 51
Dolza, John 26
Donner, Frederic 51
drivetrain 99

E

Earl, Harley 7, *8*, 8–11, 28, 36, 41
electronic control module (ECM) 89, 92
emissions laws 75, 78
engines 34 '53 14
'68 72
big-block 63-4, 72, 74, 79
Blue Flame 7, 12, 13, 14
"Californicated" 87, *90*
fuel injection (FI) 30, *38, 39*, 92, 102, *102, 103*
fuel-injection V-8 25, 27, *39*
Grand Sport 377-cid 51
L48 79
L71 66
L81 89
L82 83
L83 92
L88 67, 74
L98 105, 113
LS-7 75
LT5 *110, 111, 112*, 113
LT-1 74
Mark IV big-block *65*, 66
overheating 72, 73

pushed-back 11
Ramjet 27
smallblock 19, 63-4, *74*, 79
turbo *98*, 110
Turbo-Fire V-8 21, 22
V-6 95, *97*, 110
V-8 13, 19-21, 42, 95, *99*, 110
ZL1 74
Eschebach, Kenny 48
Estes, Pete 68

F

Fangio, Juan 42
fastback 82
fenders 68, 71
Ferrari BB512 Boxer 103
FIA 48
fiberglass 9, 15
Fitch, John *23*, 24, 35, 40, 43
Ford GT-40 *53*
Ford Motor Company 20
frame 42, 73 ladder 54, 56, *60*
fuel injection 26–7, *27*, 92 *see also* engines
"Fuelie" 25

G

gears *see* transmission
Girdler, Allan 74
glass reinforced plastic (GRP) 9, *9*
GM Art & Colour/Styling/Design 8, 77
Grand Sport 50-1, *51*
grilles *22*, 27
Grossman, Bob 35
GT cars 48

H

Haga, Hank 71
Hall, Jim 53
hand laying 15
handling 18, 22, 62, *82*, 94, 98 116
hardtops 23, *24*, *112, 113*
hatchback 59
headlights 23, 30, 58, *108*
Heberling, George 74
Heinzman, Ed 45
Holls, Dave 71
horsepower 25, 34, 38, 62, 64, 66, 80, 81
rating 76
Hotchkiss drive 13

I

independent rear suspension (IRS) 54-5
Indy 117, *118*
instrument panel 83
interior 22, 71, 72, 80
layout 30
space 72, 73

J

Jaguar XK-120 *11*
Jordan, Chuck 99

K

Keating, Thomas W. 12
Kelley, E.H. 19
Knudsen, Semon E. (Bunkie) 48, 51, 52

L

La Salle 8
Laughlin, Gary 38
layout 11, 50
mid-engine 94 *see also* interior
Le Mans 34, 42
legroom 11
LeSabre 8

M

MacKichan, Clare 11, 41, 45
McLean, Robert 9-11, 45
McLellan, David R. 81, *83*, 94, 95
magnesium 42
Mako Shark *36, 70*
Mako Shark II 69, *69, 71, 121*
Manta Ray *70*
Maserati *11*
matched-metal-die production 16
Mecom, John 52, 53
Mercedes-Benz 26
Mitchell, Bill 28, 32, 35-8, 44-6, 56, 58, 68
Mitchell ducktail *35*, 37
models 120-3
35th Anniversary *107*
'53 9-16, *10*
'54 *16*, 18–20, *20*
'55 *16*, 20-1
'56 22-5, *23, 24*, 26, *120, 124*
'57 *26*, 27-8, *27, 33, 120*
'58 28-31, *30*

'59 *22, 32*
'60 32-5, *34*
'61 35-9, *35, 36*
'62 *124*
'63 *8,* 54-62, *55, 56, 58, 59, 60*
'64 62-4
'65 64-6
'66 66
'67 66-7, *121*
'68 *71,* 71-3, *72*
'69 73-4, *73, 74*
'70 74-5, *75, 121*
'71 76, *76*
'72 76-7, *76, 77*
'73 77-8, *78, 122*
'75 79-81, *80, 81*
'76 81-2, *82, 122*
'77 82, *84*
'78 82-5, *84, 85, 89, 122*
'79 85, *87*
'80 85-9
'81 91-2, *91*
'83 94-100
'84 100-2, *100*
'85 *100,* 102-3, *103*
'88 *106, 107, 125*
'89 *111, 122, 128*
Astro *117*
Collector Edition 92, *92, 93*
Corvette Challenge *116,* 117, *125*
Grand Sport 50-1, *51, 52, 53*
Indy 117, *118*
Le Mans '60 *33*
racing 40-53
SR-2 *28,* 28, *29, 124*
SS 28, 41-44, *41-45*
X-car *95,* 95
XP-46 41
XP-64 44
XP-700 31, *35,* 36
XP-720 54
XP-880 *117*
XP-895 *80*
ZRI 110, *111,* 115, *122*
Momo, Alfred 34
Monterey Historic Races 38, *40*
Morrison, Robert S. 16
Moss, Stirling 42
Motorama 8, 15, *18*
Motorama Corvette *13,* 14
Mule 42, 43, 44, 48

N
Nassau *50,* 52
Nomad *20*

O
Olley, Maurice *9,* 12, 19
Opel Sports Car 12
options, de-proliferated 75
overdrive 99
Owens-Corning team, 74, *74, 124*

P
Pace Car 84-5
Paterson, Robert 53
Penske, Roger 53
performance 18, 21, 24, 38, 66, 72-3, 74, 110, 115, *see also* acceleration
Pontiac 48
"Porcupine" 63
Premo, Ellis J. (Jim) 15, 63
pressure-bag system 16
price 11, 15, 25, 31, 73, 74, 80, 82, 84, 90, 92, 115
production 18, 38, 61, 72, 79, 81, 82, 89, 123
10,000 mark 34

Q
Q-Corvette 32, 45, 54, 56
quality control 61, 72

R
racing 23-5, 30, 34-5, 38, 40-53, 74, 116-17
AMA ban 38, *41,* 44, 48
factory-supported 38
successes 124-5
rear axle 22, 26, 31, 42, 55, 80, 87
ride 34
Riverside 61
roof convertible 80, 103
T-top *78,* 92
targa 98
twin-bubble 36

roof panels *78*
RPO 684 28
RPO 686 31, 32
RPO ZRI 110
running gear 97, *97*
Rybicki, Irv 99

S
safety standards 75
Saginaw steering box 13
sales 18, 21, 25, 27, 31, 54, 78, 82
Chevrolet 6
policy 16
Schaafsma, Fred 98
Schemansky, Joe 11
Schinella, John 68
seams, bonding 99
seats *106*
Sebring 24–5, *25,* 28, 40
Shelby, Carroll 28, 38, 43, 51, 61
Shinoda, Larry 45, 56, 68, 71
side exhausts 64
Silver Anniversary package 84, *85*
Skelton, Betty 24
slalom times, 82, 83
Sloan, Alfred P. Jr. 8
split window *55,* 58
spoilers 85, *89*
sports cars, European 6
springs 55, 62, 90
fiberglass 97
transverse *56*
sprung weight 55
SR-2, 28, *28,* 124
SS 28, 41-44, *41-45*
steel, HSLA 96
steering ratio 13
Sting Ray 45-51, 54-68
Stingray 68-92
styling 99
'63 model 56–9
suspension 50-1, 54, 72, 97, 102

T
Taruffi, Piero 43
Thompson, Dick 28, 45, *47*
Thompson, Jerry 74
Thunderbird 20-1, *21,* 28

tires 97, 102, *111,* 115
radial 77, 83
top, folding 22
Trans-Am *116*
transaxle 32
transmission 20, 22, 61, 72, 92, 98
gearing 27, 92
manual 20
ZF *111*
Powerglide 14
Tritt, Bill 9
Tuned Port Injection (TPI) 102, *102, 103*
Turbo-Fire Corvette 21

V
vacuum-bag process 15
valet switch 115
valve system 43
vents 59, 78

W
weight 42, 55, 64, 72, 87, 102
distribution 56, 74
wheelbase 56
wheels 105, *108*
covers *7*
Woodhill Wildfire 9

X
X-car *95,* 95
XP-46 41
XP-700 31
XP-700 31
XP 895 *80*
XP-720 56
XP-895 *80*
XP-987GT *96*

Y
Young, Alan 71, *72*

Z
Z51 package 105, *106*
Z06 61, *62, 124*
ZRI 110-16, *111, 122*

ACKNOWLEDGEMENTS

The author would like to thank the following for their invaluable assistance in preparing this book: John Amgwert, Michael B. Antonick, Zora Arkus-Duntov, Richard Bak, Kurtis Bosacki, Sheila Buff, Jerry Burton, Chevrolet Public Relations, Corvette Quarterly Magazine, Cindy Cunningham, Kathy Davis, Shari (S.A.) Ferdun, Brian Goode, Craig Haase, Michael Hohn, Wade Hoyt, International Motor Sports Association, Joseph Joffe, Michael Lamm, Robert Lamm, Ed Lechtzin, Lintas:CECO Communications, Michael Bruce Associates, Jose (Joe) Morada, National Corvette Restorers Society, Lowell Paddock, Karen Penn, Kari St. Antoine, John Schinella, Robert Scott, Larry Shinoda, Sports Car Club of America, Mark Terapelli, Sonny Tippe, Rick Voegelin, Brian Wilson.

The author would especially like to thank Karl Ludvigsen for his exceptional *Corvette: America's Star Spangled Sports Car*, Mike Antonick and Michael Bruce Associates for their many Corvette publications, Michael Lamm for *The Newest Corvette*, and the men and women who have reviewed and discussed Corvettes through the years in *Motor Trend, Car & Driver, Road & Track, Car Life, Autoweek, Sports Car Graphic* and *Hot Rod*.

1989 CONVERTIBLE *Six speeds, two tops, no waiting.*